Advance Praise for *Creative Provinces—A New World of Enchanting and Empowered Communities*

With the author's grace and humor and the accompanying beautiful artwork this "how to" for a better world can be *the handbook for a magnificent future. I highly recommend this!*
          Walter Gurbo, Artist, *The Village Voice* and other venues

Creative Provinces is built around *an extraordinarily creative idea,* and Haynes delivers *a wealth of innovative examples that will enthrall her audience.*
          BookLife Prize Review

I have never read a book that encompasses so much individual imagination and envisioning – over a lifetime – than "Creative Provinces".
          Suzanne Beddoe, Creative and Performing Artist; Nurse Practitioner and Chaplain, ret., MSEd, MSN

Haynes offers *a thorough and well-structured blueprint for establishing unique, sustainable communities* grounded in heritage and innovation … [and] has done almost all of the preliminary heavy lifting in this *thoughtful and innovative guide. Very highly recommended.*
          Jamie Michele, *Readers' Favorite* 5-Star Review

Modern living is quite often monotonous and hectic. *This book will help you build your own Shangri-la. Highly recommended!*
          Pikasho Deka, *Readers' Favorite* 5-Star Review

A fascinating study of developing alternative communities that are more compatible and sustainable to its citizens. One example that Haynes gives us is *creating a real Santa's North Pole. Think of the incredibly fabulous things we could do with that!*
          Jody Hughes, Santa Claus of Butternut Valley, New York

The only hope for Humanity is to have small, self-sustaining communities with a visionary center, and Haynes gives us a foundation for doing this. *Her artful description of the many creative possibilities for ways to live together in the future belongs on the bookshelf of every creative person.*

    Dean Roberts, entrepreneur of three manufacturing businesses and author of *I'll Fix My Head Before I'm Dead*, and other books

Haynes vividly describes what inspired her to spend many years working on *the innovative ideas developed in this beautiful and startling book*

    Ginnah Howard, Author of *Night Navigation* and other books

The concept suggested in this book is a call to awaken one's inner dreams, but an effort that is not easily achievable without a hope and perseverance necessary to achieve the desired "creative province." As in Granges that came into being post-Civil War, it only came about when individuals…found each other and found strength in numbers. *It starts with a dream and the perseverance of at least one, to plant it with others who may have the same dream, and a new reality will be born.*

    Roger Halbert, Past Secretary and Vice President of New York State Grange, and Past Membership Director for the National Grange

Creative Provinces is *an impressive work of original thinking* about communities people might like to form and live in…a book that frees the imagination to consider what our perfect spot in the world might look like. *I recommend it as a highly thought-provoking resource.*

    Forrest Bachner, Author of *The Colour of the Times —Margaret Shippen Arnold and the American Revolution*

Valerie Haynes' Creative Provinces proposes *a most daring and timely concept of living deliberately and passionately* in communities of our own choosing… Haynes makes us think about how we earnestly desire to live. *When we desire it enough, we will make it happen, and Haynes' vision will be there for us.*

    Gary Norman, Anthropologist, clergy, historian

CREATIVE PROVINCES

CREATIVE PROVINCES

A New World of Enchanting and Empowered Communities

BY

VALERIE ANN LARSON HAYNES

ILLUME

Creative Provinces: A New World of Enchanting Communities,
Copyright © 2025 by Valerie Ann Larson Haynes
All rights reserved.

ISBN: 979-8-9887357-4-8

www.creativeprovinces.com

Art Credits:
Front cover image: Medieval Knights on Horseback,
stock.adobe.com/Snowshill
Back cover image: Lisa @ Pexels.com
Cover design by Kip Ayers Illustration, www.kipayersillustration.com
Book design by Cristian Radu, www.behance.net/blupage
"Balloon Glow" by Nicky Boehme
"Mt. Eaton Wayne Co. Ohio Barn Raising," Doyle Yoder Photography
"Product of the Environment" by Walter Gurbo
"Bridge Over Willow River" by Linda Cook DeVona
"Camelot Ladies of the Round Table," "Guardian,"
and "The Dixie Flagler" by Betty Ann Fraley
"Wisdom Builds Her House," by Jane Evelynne Higgins
"The Battle of the Sea" by Marjory Harris
"Adam Receives Divine Creative Inspiration" by Vance A. Larson

Printed in the United States of America

Illume Publications
An Imprint of

Illume Writers & Artists

PO Box 86
Gilbertsville, New York 13776
www.illumewritersartists.com

*Dedicated to our Ancestors, and to the Future Generations
who will honor and improve upon their creations.*

PREFACE

A Passion Long Held

When I was a child my great love was Nature. We lived on the outskirts of Minneapolis, Minnesota, which, in the 1950s, was still a vast region of lakes and wild places despite the specter of suburban development. My twin brother Vance, and I, and a few friends and our dogs, played in its endless forests, meadows, marshes, and streams. In the woods we made clearings and fashioned huts, tree houses, and villages; in the winter we made snow forts and explored the lake shores on our skates. Journeying these wilds we pretended we were Sioux Indians—living as the brothers and sisters of Nature and her creatures.

I especially loved a magnificent pond that was nestled in a clearing behind our house. It teemed with life: frogs, salamanders, toads, turtles, snakes, fish, dragonflies, butterflies, and birds. Every day we spent time there, observing its creatures in all their stages and activities. I learned more about Nature from that pond than in all the books I ever read.

But while Nature was my love, my passion was something else entirely: Every day when I came home, whether it was from a day outside or in school, I took out my ruler and some paper and created drawings and plans of all kinds of places to live: ranches, farms, and estates complete with outbuildings and landscaping. There were houses with ponds and streams; dwellings made of living trees; structures with odd shapes; and always there was something special: towers, stables, ballrooms, cat walks, Tarzan-like tree swings, horse trails, wild gardens—any fun thing I could think of. Accompanying these I wrote out plans necessary to achieve these visions.

As I grew older, I was driven to organize other matters, too: people, places, activities. It was truly a passionate interest in how things should be structured. In college I studied political science, which opened-up in me, a new and even broader structural outlook.

Then, in 1983, when my husband and I were visiting my parents in Minnesota, the four of us took a road trip to the original Larson farm in Beaver Valley, outside of Valley Springs, South Dakota. The farm was homesteaded by my great-grandparents, John Alfred Larson and Maria Nilsdotter, after they had immigrated to America from Sweden in 1869 and married. It was heartbreaking to hear my father again tell how, during the Great Depression, the family had lost the farm they had built from scratch, and had worked for over 60 years.

Returning to Minnesota, we drove by our old house where my beloved pond had nestled in the back. My father casually mentioned that the pond had been bulldozed to build another suburban neighborhood. That beautiful pool of life, which had sustained me in childhood—destroyed. Why couldn't they have built around it? And I was becoming aware that our bulldozed pond was the tip of an iceberg of senseless destruction taking place all over the world.

As my husband and I returned to our home in Virginia in heavy airline and road traffic, I wondered: Why did these things have to happen? Why did families have to lose their farms? Why did Nature have to be bulldozed? Why did the Native Americans, whose culture as children we had pretended to be a part of, have to get subsumed by the European immigrants? And why did we have to endure this blasted network of bumper-to-bumper cars!

I saw that these and other problems of the world—perhaps even all of them—were structural in nature. And if that were true, then we could create a structure to alleviate and prevent such problems. Such a structure would need to allow people to live the lives they really wanted, including all the wonderful things they could imagine: enchanting places to live; fun places where they would work at what they loved; quaint roads and billowy airways on which to travel; and magnificent cultures and communities that could also help us preserve Nature, keep peace, and live healthy lifestyles.

Shortly after we returned home I formed the idea of Creative Provinces, and for the better portion of my adult life—in my spare time from my other work—I have written and collected ideas for it and refined the concept ...My childhood passion coming to fruition.

Valerie Ann Larson Haynes
Gilbertsville, New York
2025

The author with her father, John Bertrand Larson, in 1983, on the property of the original Larson family farm homestead, Valley Springs, South Dakota.
Photo by Major General Fred E. Haynes, USMC

CONTENTS

Preface: A Passion Long Held / ix
Introduction: We Can Create a Magnificent World... / xv
Part 1: The Eight Principles of Creative Provinces / 1

    INTRODUCTION TO PART 1: A STRUCTURE FOR CREATING OUR COMMUNITY VISIONS / 2

    PRINCIPLE 1: CREATIVE PROVINCES ARE COMMUNITIES FORMED "FROM THE ROOTS UP," BY PEOPLE WITH A SHARED VISION GROUPING THEMSELVES AND THEIR PROPERTIES TOGETHER / 5

    PRINCIPLE 2: CREATIVE PROVINCES ARE "THE REAL THING" RATHER THAN "THE APPEARANCE OF" / 11

    PRINCIPLE 3: CREATIVE PROVINCES ARE LIMITLESS: THEY CAN HAVE ANY VISION, BE ANYWHERE, BE ANY SIZE, AND CAN GROW, SHRINK, CHANGE SHAPE, CONNECT, OVERLAP, AND FEDERALIZE / 19

    PRINCIPLE 4: CREATIVE PROVINCES HAVE HERITAGE TREASURES, WHICH ARE INTEGRAL TO THEIR REAL-LIFE EXISTENCE, AND WHICH THEY THUS APPROPRIATELY CREATE, REVIVE, APPRECIATE, MAINTAIN, PROTECT, AND USE / 27

    PRINCIPLE 5: CREATIVE PROVINCES ARE CREATIVE DEMOCRACIES / 35

    PRINCIPLE 6: CREATIVE PROVINCES ARE FREE AND OPEN WITHIN THEIR PROTECTIVE VISIONARY STRUCTURE / 41

    PRINCIPLE 7: CREATIVE PROVINCES ARE IN A COMPLEMENTARY RELATIONSHIP WITH THEIR SOVEREIGN STATES / 47

    PRINCIPLE 8: CREATIVE PROVINCES HOLD TO THE HIGHEST PRINCIPLES OF CREATING COMMUNITY LIFE AS A MAGNIFICENT, BEAUTIFUL, AND LOVING ART FORM / 55

    A REVIEW OF THE OCTAVE / 61

Part 2: The Four Types of Creative Provinces, with Examples / 63

    INTRODUCTION TO PART 2: THE FOUR BASIC TYPES OF CREATIVE PROVINCES / 64

    I. TRANSPORTATION AND TRAVELWAYS PROVINCES / 65

        Animal Transportation and Travelways Provinces / 67
        Pedestrian Transportation and Travelways Provinces / 71
        Motor Vehicle Transportation and Travelways Provinces / 74

Rail Transportation and Travelways Provinces / 77
Air Transportation and Travelways Provinces / 80
Water Transportation and Travelways Provinces / 83
Combined Transportation and Travelways Provinces / 86

II. INDUSTRY PROVINCES / 89
Farm and Cottage Industry Provinces / 91
Open Range, and Wild Fish, Game, and Gathering Provinces / 97
Working Animal Provinces: Giving Animals Back Their Jobs / 101
Manufacturing Provinces / 104
Education and Research Provinces / 107
Health Provinces / 109

III. ENVIRONMENT PROVINCES / 112
Garden Provinces / 113
Environmental Concept Provinces / 117
Environmental Restoration and Preservation Provinces / 121
Featured Animal Provinces / 125
Energy Provinces / 131

IV. CULTURAL PROVINCES / 134
Historic and Heritage Culture Provinces / 136
Cultural-Concept and Fantasy Provinces / 150
Artistic and Architectural Concept Provinces / 155
Relationship and Life Stages Provinces / 160
Philosophical, Religious, and Spiritual Provinces / 164
Economic Concept Provinces / 167

Part 3: Five Steps to Building a Creative Province / 171

INTRODUCTION TO PART 3: BRINGING YOUR VISION TO LIFE / 172
I. CREATE YOUR PRIMARY VISION / 173
II. CREATE SUPPORTING VISIONS TO FURTHER SHAPE YOUR PROVINCE / 179
III. CREATE RULES TO PROTECT YOUR VISION / 202
IV. ACCUMULATE AND CHRONICLE YOUR HERITAGE TREASURES / 211
V. ACTIVATE YOUR PROVINCE WITH REAL, LIVE ACTIVITIES / 222

Conclusion / 231
Acknowledgements / 233
About the Author / 235

INTRODUCTION

We Can Create a Magnificent World...

...in which any of the cultures from our heritage we want, can once again exist: the Tribal Nations, Victorian England, the Wild West, Classical Greece, the Vikings...

And we can create new cultures and communities of breathtaking beauty and joy, where Space Cities, Camelot, Shangri-la, Middle Earth, and Santa's North Pole... all really exist!

We are not talking virtual reality or theme park. This is real.

Enough of boring, mass-market monoculture. Do you long to live in a unique, magical community? Or to restore your ancestral heritage? Do you daydream of the beauty and romance of a bygone era, or of living in a garden paradise? Well, pine away no more. You can easily create the world you've always dreamed of having!

You can create lands of castles and knights in shining armor. You can have space cities with ports to other worlds. You can recreate the great camel caravan trade routes and the ancient walled cities of the Arabian Peninsula. You can recreate Roaring 1920's towns complete with speakeasies, flappers, and antique cars. You can have Motown. Ancient Alexandria. You can have the rustic living of Old Hawaii. You can recreate the Ming Dynasty for crying out loud. You can, in fact, create or recreate just about anything you want.

Perhaps you long for the return of your heritage language, costumes, and traditions, or to go back to the refined days or excitement of a previous time—but the world keeps telling you "you can't go back." Well, nonsense! You *can* go back, and furthermore, you can make it *even better* than before. The Old South can have all the graciousness of the Nineteenth Century—but this time with an equally gracious alternative to slavery. Medieval Europe can exist again, but this time with a friendlier version of the Inquisition! And the Roman Empire can be revived in all its imperialistic glory—but with invasions that are a lot more fun!

Are you fed up with being ineffective as the environment continues to be wrecked by out-of-control technology and development? Well, say sayonara to *that* reality. Not only can you establish protected wildernesses, large and small, but you can make them enchanting paradises in which to not only visit but to live. Or suppose you'd prefer not to be bombarded with invasive, health-damaging electromagnetic frequencies everywhere you stepped. You can create communities that not only have safe technologies, but quaintly so!

And the endless choke-hold of automobile traffic? Whoa! You can leave *that* reality behind in the dust. You can create vast networks of horse roads, bicycles arteries, camel caravans, vintage automobile towns and roads, and antique and futuristic rail lines, all of which meander around the globe, connecting similar enchanting communities.

Are you steaming mad over big corporations having gotten away with cut-throat tactics that put you out of business... and you long to return to small, locally-run shops and farms, and traditional local industries? Well, guess what? *You have the power to take it all back*! You can easily create agricultural regions made up of hundreds—heck, thousands—of small family farms and cottage industries; or vast networks of independent seaport villages where men fish in the old tradition. And wouldn't it be wonderful to recreate vast open ranges for herding cattle, and hunting with dogs and falcons, and not have to worry about them getting flattened by diesel trucks? Surprise! You can have it!

Maybe you've fallen into the limited mindset that says that planes and drones own the sky. Think again. You can create peaceful valleys where air travel is by balloon. And wouldn't a spaceport city be phenomenal? A high-tech futuristic city run by scientists, and filled with space art, where you catch rocket ships to other planets.

And wait, there's so much more! How about a city of choruses where everyone sings during feasts in great dining halls? Or a water city filled with intricate canals, elaborate fountains, gorgeous waterfowl, and vast fleets of interesting boats! Or cat-friendly walk-street neighborhoods with elaborate aerial catwalks and midnight tomcat serenades.

Or how about a community that is *enchantingly* off-grid—such as one not only *with its own* natural gas source, but also gas street lamps, gas-lit homes, T. S. Eliott readings, and carriages pulled by horses that steam and stamp.

Or maybe you simply wish you could escape the constant racket of loud motors and somebody else's annoying music, but can't afford your own island. Good news: You can easily establish neighborhoods, regions, lakes—whatever—that have beautiful and creative soundscapes.

Sure, all this is wonderful, you're probably thinking—but how in the world do we do it? Well, prepare yourself, because the answer is surprisingly simple: You *provincialize.*

> *Creative Provinces are communities established for the creation or reclamation of a unique culture, travelway, industry, or environment by people organized as a group of properties.*

Creative Provinces are communities people can create—in which to live, work, or travel—anywhere, beginning with their own private properties. First you decide how you want to live; then you organize your property with the properties of others with a similar vision. Over time, hubs form, as people connect or relocate to where their visions are being manifested. It's an *organic* process.

Part One of this book lays out the eight principles of Creative Provinces. Part Two gives many ideas for different types of Creative Provinces. And Part Three gives basic guidance on starting a Creative Province.

My sincere hope is that this book inspires and empowers you to create the lives you have always dreamed of living.

Definitions of Creative Province Terms

The word "province" has traditionally been used to designate places that are under the purview of certain governments and organizations, as well as bodies of knowledge under the purview of particular schools of thought. Our use of the word "province" further evolves from this. Used in our context, a Creative Province refers to a place that forms where people with similar visions connect themselves and their properties together to create a community of a unique culture, travelway, industry, or environment. Thus:

Creative Provinces are places where people have connected themselves and their properties together to create a community vision—specifically, the creation or reclamation of a unique culture, travelway, industry, or environment.

To Provincialize is to establish such a Creative Province.

Provincials are people who are members of such Creative Provinces.

People can also use the more specific terms, examples of which are given in Part Two of this book, to indicate Creative Provinces. Such specific terms will be particularly helpful in Sovereign States where the term "province" is already used to designate an administrative region.

Transportation Provinces are Creative Provinces that have a Transportation concept as their primary vision.

Travelways Provinces are Creative Provinces that have a Travelway as their primary vision.

Industry Provinces are Creative Provinces that have an Industry as their primary vision.

Environment Provinces are Creative Provinces that have an Environmental concept as their primary vision.

Cultural Provinces are Creative Provinces that have a Cultural concept as their primary vision.

Part I

THE EIGHT PRINCIPLES OF CREATIVE PROVINCES

PRINCIPLE ONE: Creative Provinces Are Communities Formed "From the Roots Up," By People With a Shared Vision Grouping Themselves and Their Properties Together / *4*

PRINCIPLE TWO: Creative Provinces Are "The Real Thing" Rather Than "The Appearance Of" / *10*

PRINCIPLE THREE: Creative Provinces Are Limitless: They Can Have Any Vision, be Anywhere, be Any Size, and Can Grow, Shrink, Change Shape, Connect, Overlap, and Federalize / *18*

PRINCIPLE FOUR: Creative Provinces Have Heritage Treasures, Which Are Integral to Their Real-Life Existence, and Which They Thus Appropriately Create, Revive, Appreciate, Maintain, Protect, and Use / *26*

PRINCIPLE FIVE: Creative Provinces Are Creative Democracies / *34*

PRINCIPLE SIX: Creative Provinces Are Free and Open Within Their Protective Visionary Structure / *40*

PRINCIPLE SEVEN: Creative Provinces Are in a Complementary Relationship with Their Sovereign States / *46*

PRINCIPLE EIGHT: Creative Provinces Hold to the Highest Principles of Creating Community Life as a Magnificent, Beautiful, and Loving Art Form / *54*

Introduction to Part 1

A Structure for Creating Our Community Visions

There is nothing like a dream to create the future.

—Victor Hugo

Creating and following a Vision is the most powerful thing you can do to have the life you want. And the Creative Province structure enables people to *collectively* create and follow a Vision to have the lives they want—the cultures, travelways, industries, and environments—and maintain their integrity. By connecting themselves and their properties as Creative Provinces, people can create places to live, work, and travel, in ways that suit their most magnificent visions.

The construct throughout history has often been that only the rich and powerful can create the lives they want, which they accomplish by hiring a lot of poorer people to make it happen. This construct has created many beautiful things, but at a great spiritual cost, in that huge numbers of people never live the lives they truly want. People have often tried to amend this situation through their governments, but with poor and even disastrous results.

And in recent times we've been dominated by yet another vision of a few wealthy individuals: a globalist, technocratic, big-corporate future that will have most people living in "smart cities" with the likes of artificial intelligence, micro-chipped bodies, the "Internet of Things," drones, driverless cars, and a countryside dominated by factory farms and vast agri-business monoculture fields of genetically modified crops grown with artificial fertilizers and pesticides.

But is this the vision of the future *everyone* wants? *Definitely not!*

In addition to this limited vision of the future, many of us have been mired in a limited mindset that says we can't change the world—that we can't go back to a more graceful time; that there's nothing we can do about technological changes; that we are powerless against the tide of modernity; that we must compromise our vision; that only big money can create wonderful things; that the Earth is doomed; and so on. *But none of this is true.* We just need the structural tools to empower ourselves to create the world we want.

The Creative Province structure is such a tool. It enables us to create communities based on our visions of how we truly want to live, and to maintain their integrity. With Creative Provinces, we can create the lifestyles we want, and not have them be exposed to every kind of outside cultural expression imaginable, as if our creations were canvases upon which anyone can splatter paint.

Part One of this book lays out the Eight Principles of Creative Provinces—the framework for living that will allow us to manifest these dreams.

American Winter Scenes: Evening, Frances F. Palmer, 1854, Currier & Ives lithograph with hand coloring

PRINCIPLE 1: CREATIVE PROVINCES ARE COMMUNITIES FORMED "FROM THE ROOTS UP," BY PEOPLE WITH A SHARED VISION GROUPING THEMSELVES AND THEIR PROPERTIES TOGETHER

Like Nature, communities thrive from the roots up, not the other way around.

—HRH, the Prince of Wales, *Harmony: A New Way of Looking at Our World*

CREATIVE PROVINCES ARE COMMUNITIES FORMED "FROM THE ROOTS UP" BASED ON A SHARED VISION

The first principle of Creative Provinces is that they are communities formed "from the roots up," by people with a shared vision grouping themselves and their properties together to create cultures, travelways, industries, and environments.

Creative Provinces are thus groups of people who share a Vision that they want to manifest into a physical community. They are thus a type of "intentional community"—a community based on a shared vision.

It is the shared-vision principle that differentiates Creative Provinces and other intentional communities, from all other types of physical communities (which we may call "non-intentional" communities), such as sovereign states, cities, and villages, which have a heterogeneous population with many different visions and reasons for living there.

These "non-intentional" communities may attempt to create a cohesive Vision for their population using such devices as zoning ordinances, or a "comprehensive plan," or a state religion. But such "from the top down" attempts to create a cohesive vision for a heterogeneous settlement must be either very watered-down with all manner of compromises, or the vision must be forced upon people who do not share it. Thus the members of these non-intentional communities cannot truly live according to their own community visions—they must compromise.

But does community living always have to involve compromising our visions? Absolutely not! We can exercise our Community Visions by aligning ourselves with others who share those visions.

Creative Provinces Are Intentional Communities – the Next Generation

There are many intentional communities of varying sorts that exist today, such as retirement communities, eco-villages, co-housing communities, and religious-order communities. They all begin with a shared vision. But most of them are also limited in many ways, usually in that they have a certain piece of property that the members have to "buy into."

Creative Provinces, in contrast, are unlimited, for many reasons described in the subsequent principles, but especially because they are based on the private ownership of individual properties. Thus, instead of an already existing property with set boundaries that people buy into, the individual properties of Creative Provinces fit together like Lego blocks, building a community.

These individually owned properties can be owned by singular individuals, or by groups of people, such as private companies, non-profit groups, churches, or even government entities.

The current intentional communities, however, can be said to be *proto*-Creative-Provinces. Put another way, Creative Provinces can be said to be "intentional communities—the next generation."

Grouping Properties Together Gives a Vision a Place in Which To Manifest As a Community

This brings up the question: Why create communities that include our properties; why not just form clubs of people with similar visions? The answer is fundamental:

Property gives a vision a place in which to manifest. And multiple properties give a vision a place in which to manifest as a community.

For example, people who belong to a historical society, and who themselves might variously own and control houses and other buildings built in the 1700s, might form an Eighteenth Century Province, with the vision of creating a place where the culture, environment, industries, and travelways of that era are revived. Each of these provincials would maintain legal ownership of their own property, but the Creative Province would include these properties in its visionary plan in order to manifest period lifestyles and activities, such as horse travel, non-electric households, period music, dance, costume, and manners. And so instead of just a historical society with a few museums, tours, and other passive activities, there is now a place where the historical lifestyle and culture of the Eighteenth Century actually exists.

CREATIVE PROVINCES EXERCISE DEMOCRACY WITH COMMUNITY VISIONS

Thus we can declare our property vision and group our properties together with others with the same property vision.

Those of us who have a cultural, travelway, industry, or environment vision can declare ourselves and our property as a Creative Province with that particular vision. Others, who share that vision, can then join the Province and include themselves and their property in it. These properties connect as people add themselves and their property to the Province. Some people will also buy property and relocate to where their vision is being most successfully manifested.

Provincials will continue to fully own and control their individual properties, but while they are members of a Creative Province, they will follow that Province's vision. And anytime they decide they no longer want to follow that vision, they can leave the Province.

With Creative Provinces, we are thus able to declare and exercise our community visions with our own property. In this way we exercise our democracy in a totally new way—with our property visions. We are not just voting for laws administered by a governing body of a large group of various kinds of people; we are additionally voting our lifestyle visions *with our property*. This is a true upgrade in the practice of democracy.

Creative Provinces will of course be under the jurisdictions of their respective sovereign states. See Principle 7 for a description of this relationship.

Medieval Knights on Horseback, stock.adobe.com/Snowshill

Principle 2: Creative Provinces Are "The Real Thing" Rather Than "The Appearance Of"

Let us have a robust, manly life; let us know what we know, for certain; what we have, let it be solid and seasonable and our own. A world in the hand is worth two in the bush. Let us have to do with real men and women, and not with skipping ghosts.

—Ralph Waldo Emerson, *Representative Men*

WE CAN RETURN TO REAL LIVING

The second principle of Creative Provinces is that they are "The Real Thing" rather than "The Appearance Of." They are real environments where people live, work, and travel, and engage in real activities.

Creative Provinces are not virtual communities, and they are not amusement parks or theme parks. Nor are they associations or clubs where people meet periodically to discuss a common interest; nor are they reenactments where people participate in something wonderful for just a weekend. However, these activities will often be important steps to creating Provinces.

"THE APPEARANCE OF" LIVING, AND FAKERY EVERYWHERE

Today we take great pains to give *the appearance of living*.

But we are actually spending less and less of our time in Nature, in gardens, with animals, engaging in real physical work and play, and participating in community activities.

Instead, we spend more and more of our time in a technological, two-dimensional world watching screens where other people pretend to live. And then we ride around in machines going from one fake-living scenario on the screen to another. We are also getting more and more of our information and sense of reality from unknown people hidden behind these screens, and less and less from real experience.

And it is so easy to fool people in the two-dimensional world! We are buying products that *look like* "the wonderful real thing," but which actually come from unknown sources that may use highly unethical practices, such as factory sweat shops and factory farms, or which in reality are artificial products made in laboratories.

We are becoming so removed from our much-loved, wonderful and living real world, that we are barely noticing that it is being killed off and replaced with genetically modified versions, machines, robots, screens, and chemicals.

This is not to say that technology, two-dimensional information, and pretend-living are bad things—indeed they are often helpful, and even necessary *tools* to help us create the real lives we want to lead. But if they are *done to excess*, then the Machine we are riding around in will carry us right over a cliff.

Fortunately, with Creative Provinces we can reconnect with our very wonderful, Real World.

RESONANCE—THE KEY TO REGAINING AND MAINTAINING HEALTH AND REAL LIVING

The universal principle of Resonance means that what you put out to the Universe—your actions to people, animals, and Nature; what kind of food you grow, buy, and eat; and your thoughts and attitudes—you resonate with it, and it becomes your own personal reality.

There are many versions of this universal principle. The *Bible* and other spiritual texts are replete with calls to "do unto others as you would do unto yourself." This universal maxim, "the Golden Rule," means more than kindness. What you do and say becomes your reality.

Here is an everyday example: Native Americans hunted buffalo and led extremely active lives in the natural world, as do all hunter-gatherer people. In contrast, people who eat diets of factory-farmed meat, eggs, and dairy from animals which are so confined they never see the Sun or graze in a pasture, themselves lead inactive lives of confinement indoors looking at screens. Another example: People who eat foods grown with poisons, themselves develop disease. And another: It is no coincidence that the wearing of masks has accompanied censorship—the "muzzling" of free speech. These are just a few illustrations of how resonance works.

So—the first and most important step in regaining a full, healthy *real life*, is to be sure you buy, eat, and use products that are ethically, humanely, and naturally produced, and to be aware of how what you are doing is resonating with your world. To be successful using the principles in this book you must bring your own spiritual resonance to a place of real, harmonious living with those lives (human, animal, and vegetable) you encounter.

Creative Provinces are Places of Real Living

Creative Provinces are places where people *truly live* their fondest dreams. They enable people to activate their aliveness in infinite ways, by creating and recreating real, human-scaled, and life-enhancing activities—in communities, industries, environments, and travelways of wonder and enchantment. Thus:

- Instead of studying ancient history in books, on the computer, or in classrooms...
  ...Learning ancient history by living in an ancient city, speaking its language, living its culture, and participating in its events.
- Instead of sitting inertly in an audience watching musicians, singers, and dancers...
  ...Dancing at grand balls, country dances, and night clubs, singing in dining halls, and gathering with your friends at elegant soirees.
- Instead of massive, mechanized superships that put fishermen out of work and decimate the oceans...
  ...Coastal communities of small-craft, independent fishermen, fishing in the old tradition.
- Instead of unhealthy and inhumane factory farms...
  ...Real pastoral countryside with grazing animals and cowboys on horseback herding cattle.
- Instead of being manipulated into a genocidal and ecocidal vortex of computerized, so-called "modern warfare"...
  ...Real men fighting with agreed-upon and honorably chosen weapons, in real physical battles.
- Instead of endless lawns mowed with machines...
  ...Herds of sheep shepherded by shepherds and border collies.
- Instead of mass-produced products made in distant and out-of-sight factory sweatshops...

...Quaint villages filled with artisans making and selling their own crafts.
- Instead of touring museums, historic homes, and ruins, and watching old movies and daydreaming of the romance and excitement of yesterday...
  ...Living in real heritage communities that preserve the period dress, manners, language, traditions, art, and other treasures, and keeping alive their heritage activities.
- Instead of visiting fantasy theme parks...
  ...Participating in real, magical communities where fantasy characters truly exist, live, and work.
- Instead of driving to work or to a gym in heavy traffic...
  ...Pedaling everywhere on vast networks of bicycle roads.
- Instead of poisons and traps killing off rodents and insects...
  ...Cats prowling the neighborhood, and bats filling the skies at night, all hunting to feed themselves as nature intended.
- Instead of alarms and electronic tracking devices...
  ...Watchdogs and tracking-dogs doing the work they love to do.
- Instead of endangered wildlife languishing in zoos...
  ...Wildlife thriving in wildernesses and wildlife corridors, with zoologists and nature lovers living there who help maintain the wildlife.
- Instead of sending your money to an environmental organization to "save a wilderness"...
  ...Becoming a part of a wilderness where you live and physically help to revive it.
- Instead of trying to find a date on a computer screen and ending up having your identity stolen, or worse...
  ...Being part of a heritage community, where the families know each other, and people follow courtship customs.
- Instead of watching a few millionaires playing sports on television...
  ...Managing, coaching, refereeing, playing in, and cheering your own Creative Province's teams.

This list literally has no end. Creative Provinces are a way for people to not only regain real, genuine living, but to do so in the most fun and enchanting ways imaginable.

CREATIVE PROVINCES ARE THE GENUINE REAL THING COME TO LIFE

In addition to having real activities, Creative Provinces are the Genuine, Real Thing Come to Life.

This means that Creative Provinces are not "playing at" living; they are doing it for real. This is a particularly important point with Period and Historical Provinces: They existed once in a previous time, and now they exist again, but in an appropriately altered form.

Thus a Province of Ancient Rome would be the real Rome of the Roman Empire, coming back to life like a thought-to-be-extinct creature being nurtured back to existence. The Roman Senate and the Roman Legion would be there in all their imperialistic attitude and glory. And perhaps they will be engaged in battles with provincial Vikings this time.

A Garden of Eden would be the real paradise of Genesis, meticulously restored with loving hands. And Camelot would have its real Arthur and Guinevere, the Round Table, and tournaments with jousting knights.

The same would be true with Fantasy and other Cultural Concept Provinces: The worlds of Oz, Middle Earth, Narnia, and Hogsmeade, with all the magic therein, will become real when provincials create them.

The music of Wagner will come to life in a Teutonic province, and the art of Rembrandt will come to life in an Old Dutch Province.

And Santa, the North Pole, elf toymaking, and the Polar Express all become real when we create them using our fondest, whimsical ventures.

Balloon Glow, © Nicky Boehme/Artlicensing.com

PRINCIPLE 3: CREATIVE PROVINCES ARE LIMITLESS: THEY CAN HAVE ANY VISION, BE ANYWHERE, BE ANY SIZE, AND CAN GROW, SHRINK, CHANGE SHAPE, CONNECT, OVERLAP, AND FEDERALIZE

Life is eternal; and love is immortal; and death is only a horizon; and a horizon is nothing save the limit of our sight.

—Rossiter Worthington Raymond,
A Commentary Prayer

We Can Create Infinite Places of Wonder and Enchantment

The third Principle of Creative Provinces is that they are limitless: They can have any kind of vision; they can be anywhere and encompass any area; they can be any size, and can grow, shrink, and change shape; and they can connect and overlap.

This dynamic structure allows for the limitless expression of human group creativity as people create the cultures, environments, industries, and travelways of their dreams.

Creative Provinces Can Have Any Kind of Vision, within the Laws of the Land

Creative Provinces are realms of endless creativity, wonder, and enjoyment. Every beautiful lifestyle we have sighed over, every adventurous life we have wanted to experience, every peaceful valley we have longed for, we can create; and every lost culture or other treasure we weep for, we can create anew.

Creative Province Visions can be any type of lifestyle choices people want, within the laws of the land. And if a Province is prevented from manifesting a vision because of a law, it can gain the political clout, as it grows, to change that law.

The Primary and Supporting Province Visions

Creative Provinces will have one Primary Vision that will be a succinct statement defining its main purpose. This Primary Vision will be the anchor for the Province's activities; it will be integral to the Province's name; and it will allow for the ease of its identification and categorization.

Under the Primary Vision, as many Supporting Visions as desired can be added. Supporting Visions further develop the main goal of the Province.

For example, a Sunshine Province might be created with the primary vision of being an off-grid, solar-powered community. It may then have supporting visions that state goals to encourage solar-power industries, and sunshine-related cultural activities.

Parts Two and Three of this book explain Province visions in more detail, with many examples.

Creative Provinces Can Be Any Size, Can Be Anywhere, and Can Encompass Any Area

Creative Provinces are not under the purview of sovereign states, and thus can transcend state borders, existing anywhere. Thus they can be any size, can be located anywhere, and can encompass any area. A Creative Province that starts with a few properties in one village, for example, might expand to include properties in many other villages, sovereign states, federal entities, and continents.

Creative Provinces can be as small as a section of a neighborhood, or as large as worldwide.

An Acoustic Jazz Province, for example, might exist on a particular city street. A Quiet Province might encompass the properties surrounding a small lake. And a Canary Province might be created in and around a neighborhood of apartment complexes with aviaries.

Conversely, an Ancient Province might form that includes areas surrounding the ancient monuments of Egypt, Greece, Rome, Iraq, Turkey and elsewhere, and attendant properties associated with them, eventually becoming a world-wide Province where the Ancient World is preserved and its cultures restored.

Likewise, Wilderness Provinces may form and connect throughout entire continents.

But here is a caveat: No matter the size of your Creative Province, make sure its structure is "human-scaled" and simple enough to be easily managed. See the discussion on OATS (oversight, accountability, transparency, and simplicity) in Principle 5: Creative Provinces are Creative Democracies, for more on this.

CREATIVE PROVINCES CAN GROW, SHRINK, AND CHANGE SHAPE

A Creative Province grows, shrinks, and changes shape as people join their properties to it, or remove their properties from it. Thus Creative Provinces are constantly changing in size. Keep in mind that all creations have life spans. Like any artist, when your creation has run its course—like a play or an event—create again!

This changeable nature is part of the organic process that is integral to provincial strength, and reflects the "living nature" of Creative Provinces.

For example, people who want to live in a community of wildflower meadows, natural quietude, and birdsong, can start a Birdsong Province by declaring themselves and their properties as the foundation of the Province. As more and more like-minded people sign up their properties to be part of this Birdsong Province, the Province grows, takes on its own unique shape, and becomes a reality. And as provincials leave the Province—for example, if they sell their property and move away—the Province will again change its shape and size.

CREATIVE PROVINCES CAN CONNECT, OVERLAP, AND COMBINE

CREATIVE PROVINCES CAN CONNECT VIA PROVINCE TRAVELWAYS

Creative Provinces, particularly those with similar or Complementary visions, can connect to each other via Province Travelways.

For example, various Horse Provinces and Historic and Heritage Culture Provinces might connect via Horse Roads. Bicycle Provinces might connect with bicycle paths.

A Creative Province can also have many different kinds of province travelway connections.

For example, a Hot Air Balloon Province might connect to a Bicycle Province via both hot air balloon airways and bicycle paths. The Balloon Province might also connect to a Nineteenth Century Historic and Heritage Culture Province via balloon and vintage airplane airways, horse roads, and vintage motor vehicle roads.

CREATIVE PROVINCES CAN COMBINE AND SEPARATE

Creative Provinces with similar or Complementary visions can combine to form a larger Province.

For example, a "Virginia Civil War Era Province" might join with several other Historic and Heritage Culture Provinces of that era to form a larger, "American Mid-Nineteenth Century Province."

Likewise, Province Travelways with Complementary visions might want to combine in order to expand. For example, a Pre-Industrial Historic Road Province might combine in certain places with non-historic Horse Road Provinces, in order to connect to various horse-friendly provinces.

Provinces can also separate to form two or more smaller provinces.

For example, if provincials of a Nordic Furniture Manufacturing Province feel their province has gotten too large to manage properly, they might divide into several smaller creative provinces, such as a Regin Artisan Furniture Manufacturing Province and a Viking Masters Artisan Furniture Manufacturing Province.

Or if certain provincials want to change their supporting visions, but others don't want to, they can split off to form a separate province.

For example, if a Quiet Province has supporting visions limiting equipment to a certain decibel level, but some provincials want to reduce that level even further, they could split off and form a sister province, but with a more strict version of quietude.

CREATIVE PROVINCES CAN OVERLAP

Creative Provinces, in their natural and organic development, will often overlap.

For example, part of an Organic Garden Province might exist inside a Quiet Province; and another part of it might overlap a Victorian-Era Province. Each of these, in turn, might overlap a Bicycle Road Province at different places.

CREATIVE PROVINCES CAN EXIST WITHIN OTHER CREATIVE PROVINCES

Creative Provinces can also exist partly or entirely within other Creative Provinces.

For example, an Arctic Wilderness Province, with a Primary Vision of ecologically restoring and preserving the wilderness, might eventually become a vast Creative Province. Inside of this Province there may also be many other creative provinces, including an Eskimo Province, a Reindeer Province, Santa's North Pole, a Polar Bear Province, and a Dog Sled Province Travelway.

CREATIVE PROVINCES CAN JOIN TOGETHER IN A FEDERATION

Creative Provinces with the same, similar, or Complementary visions can also join together to form Province Federations, for the purposes of sharing information and other resources.

For example, a Mother Goose Province may wish to join a Renaissance and Fantasy Province Federation for mutual benefit in expanding the magnificence of their creation.

As with individual Creative Provinces, Province Federations can overlap, and exist inside one another. Creative Provinces can also belong to many federations, and remove themselves from such federations if they so choose.

ONE WORLD, INFINITE PROVINCES, COMPRISING A LIMITLESS, LIVING CREATIVE EMPIRE

There is no end to the types of Creative provinces that can be formed. Part Two of this book gives examples of some of these, classified into four general categories: Transportation and Travelways Provinces, Industry Provinces, Environment Provinces, and Cultural Provinces.

Also described are various "proto-creative-province" communities which already exist, but which could truly blossom in the Creative Province structure.

The limitlessness of Creative Provinces can be compared to two things: 1) the infinite variety of species we find in Nature, with their ever-changing growth and migratory patterns; and 2) to a living body's microbiome.

As such, our creative provinces, combined, form Humanity's living creative empire. Indeed, we are *the* Living, Creative Empire.

Sioux Village near Fort Laramie, Albert Bierstadt, 1859

Principle 4: Creative Provinces Have Heritage Treasures, Which Are Integral to Their Real-Life Existence, and Which They Thus Appropriately Create, Revive, Appreciate, Maintain, Protect, and Use

What thou lovest well is thy true heritage.
—Ezra Pound, *Cantos*

We Can Keep Our Heritage Treasures

The fourth principle of Creative Provinces is that they have Heritage Treasures, which are integral to their real-life existence, and which they thus appropriately create, revive, appreciate, maintain, protect, and use.

The Vast Treasures of Humanity's Heritage

Humanity's treasures are vast: its knowledge, information, and languages; its history and cultures; its wildlife and natural resources; its industries with their craftsmen; its artists and other visionaries; its scientists and other experts; its domestic and trained animals; and its architecture, art, artifacts and infrastructures. These vast treasures are Humanity's Heritage.

The keepers of Humanity's Heritage Treasures are individuals and groups of many kinds. But throughout history we have seen so many of our treasures destroyed as one group stamps out or takes over another. Today this destruction continues: Globalism elbows-out local cultures and industries; various "cultural sensitivities" demand that religious and historic symbols be removed from public display; and excesses of all kinds decimate natural environments.

The Creative Province structure, however, is a powerful way Humanity can protect its Heritage Treasures and restore those that have been lost.

Creative Provinces Are Keepers of Our Heritage Treasures

Because Creative Provinces have Heritage Treasures, which they either revive or create anew, and which are integral to their real-life existence, it is incumbent upon them to appropriately appreciate, maintain, protect, and use these treasures.

When provincials join a Creative Province, they bring with them any number of Heritage Treasures, which correlate with the Province Vision, including themselves and their correlated expertise and property. Provincials retain "legal" ownership of their correlated province properties; but at the same time these are included in the aggregate Heritage Treasures of the Province.

For example, the owners of a medieval castle, when they join a Medieval Province, will bring with them, the castle, as well as their historical knowledge of the medieval period. The castle's owners will retain legal ownership of their castle; but at the same time, the Medieval Province will include among its Heritage Treasures, the castle and its historical knowledge.

Thus, a creative province will have any number of Heritage Treasures that correlate with its Vision, and which will be integral to its real-life existence. Some of these heritage treasures will change as the province membership changes, and other, non-property heritage treasures, such as knowledge and language, will stay with the province regardless of its membership fluctuations.

A Creative Province's Treasures Correlate with Its Vision

A Creative Province's Heritage Treasures are those properties and expertise of its provincials that correlate with its Vision; they do not include provincials' properties and expertise that do not thus correlate.

To use a very simple example, the Heritage Treasures of a Quiet Province would be its provincials, the land they wish to include in the Province, the natural quietude, and the provincials' expertise, personal property, and efforts that relate to maintaining the Province's natural quietude; for example, a provincial's "quiet" electric trimmer and his noise meter might be included. Any property and expertise of the provincials that did not correlate with this Province's Vision, such as the provincials' wardrobes, furniture, and musical skills, the Province would not want to include among its Heritage Treasures.

The Six Types of Creative Province Heritage Treasures

1. The Provincials

First and foremost among a Creative Province's Heritage Treasures will be its membership, its "provincials"—people dedicated to living the Province Vision. As with any organization, the membership will be the essence of the Province. Provincials will run the Province, make its decisions, and keep its Province Vision. They will provide the expertise, labor, and caring that will make the Province the special place it is meant to be.

A Province's membership will be comprised of individuals, but it may also include groups, such as non-profit organizations, businesses, and government entities. For example, the members of a non-profit battlefield park organization might vote to become part of a Historic Province, and would be member provincials. In another example, the owners and renters of a business park may vote to become part of an Athletic Province and would be member provincials. And in a third example, a sovereign state may decide to include several of its national parks in a Wilderness Corridor Province, and the officers of those national parks would be member provincials.

2. The Provincials' Real Property

Particularly significant for most Creative Provinces will be their Real Property Heritage Treasures—the correlating land and buildings of their provincials. These treasures will usually include the homes and land properties of the provincials. They will also include such real properties as grazing lands for a Cattle Province; coastline property for an Independent Fishermen's Province; key connective property for a Horse Road Province; and a collection of yellow houses and other buildings powered by solar panels in a Sunshine Province.

It will be essential for Creative Provinces to keep a current map and spreadsheet of their provincials' real properties.

3. The Province's Natural Resources

Most Creative Provinces will have Natural Resource Heritage Treasures that its member provincials will bring to the Province with their correlated land. These will be not only the physical resource treasures themselves, such as the wildlife, wildernesses, rivers, streams, and mountain ranges; but also *the integrity of* those resources, such as the cleanness and viability of the air, water, and soil; the natural quietude; and the dark night skies.

All Creative Provinces will do well to claim and chronicle the Natural Resource Heritage Treasures that in any way correlate with their Province Vision—to use, protect, honor, and celebrate.

4. THE PROVINCIALS' CORRELATED PERSONAL PROPERTY

Most Creative Provinces will have correlated personal property among their Heritage Treasures. Provincials will bring with them any number of treasures that correlate with the Province Vision, such as their art, artifacts, wardrobes, musical instruments, and domestic animals.

For example, the provincials of a Horse Province will have their horses, and also their carriages, wagons, and other equipment related to horse care and travel, all of which will count among the Province's correlated personal property Heritage Treasures. Likewise, an Acoustic Jazz Province will include the musical instruments and related equipment of its provincials among its personal property Heritage Treasures.

5. THE PROVINCE'S INDUSTRIES

Many Creative Provinces will have Industry Heritage Treasures, and some provinces will have an industry as their Primary Vision.

Thus, an Organic Cotton Province might have organic cotton farming and textile manufacturing—including its farmers and craftsmen, and their land, seed, and equipment—among its primary Industry Heritage Treasures.

In another example, a Medieval Province might include among its Heritage Treasures a medieval sporting event industry, an armor industry, and a sheep industry with grazing lands, all of which would be counted among their Province Industry Heritage Treasures.

6. THE PROVINCE'S INFORMATION, HISTORY, AND CULTURE

Among the most important Heritage Treasures of a Creative Province will be its critical and unique information, history, and culture: its aggregate knowledge, language, customs, and events, and the documentation of these.

For example, Information Heritage Treasures might include significant research and investigations. Historic Heritage Treasures might include a lost history the Province will restore. And Cultural Heritage Treasures might include a forgotten language the Province will bring back to use; provincial art, music, and dance; or a culture of costume, manners, and behavior.

Unlike the privately owned physical properties of provincials that might leave the creative province as its membership fluctuates, a province's Information, History, and Culture will always remain with a province.

Creating and Reviving Heritage Treasures

Creating provincial Heritage Treasures, or reviving those that are disappearing or have been lost, is one of the primary functions of a Creative Province. Examples include:

- Creating a new culture, with language, customs, costume, and events, or reviving a lost culture;
- Restoring a depleted environment, or creating a new environment;
- Creating a new type of transportation or reviving an old kind of transportation; and
- Creating new industries or reviving old industries.

Appreciating Heritage Treasures

Appreciating provincial Heritage Treasures is the foundation of appropriately maintaining, protecting, and using them. For this reason, one of the primary functions of a Creative Province will be to define and document its Heritage Treasures, and teach its provincials and visitors about them.

Thus, Historic and Heritage Culture Provinces will have provincials who are historians and culturists who will research, document, and teach the histories and customs of the Province; linguists who will teach the historic language; and designers, builders, and artisans who will instruct others on how to make the period buildings, fashions, and accouterments.

In another example, Environmental Restoration Provinces will have provincials who are ecologists and biologists who study and document the Provinces' environments, and teach others about restoring them.

Protecting Province Treasures

One of the most important purposes of Creative Provinces is to appropriately protect their Heritage Treasures. They will be *protectors* of their history, culture, and information. This is particularly important, because throughout history, various cultures have seen their histories and other significant information destroyed or altered by others who have a different vision and point of view.

Creative provinces will also *protect* their industries and markets. For example, an Organic Farm Province might *protect* its farms from large-corporate economic tactics through a variety of methods, including a network of cooperative marketing and distribution.

Creative provinces will also *protect* their environments and travelways. For example, a Countryside Horse Province will adopt methods to *protect* its roads and lands from motorized vehicles.

Using Province Treasures

And finally, Creative Provinces will appropriately use their Heritage Treasures, and by doing so will keep them alive.

Thus, a Hot-Air Balloon Airway will *use* its hot-air balloons as a means of travel from one point to another.

A Grandfather River Restoration Province will *use* its river in an ecologically safe manner. For example, it might promote river-friendly travel, fishing, and other activities.

And a Federation of Native American Provinces will *use* the many heritage languages and customs of the individual tribes they have revived. For example, tribes might *use* their heritage hunting and gathering methods for subsistence, and they might *use* their heritage abodes by living in them.

Camelot Ladies of the Round Table, © Betty Ann Fraley

PRINCIPLE 5: CREATIVE PROVINCES ARE CREATIVE DEMOCRACIES

Whoso pulleth out this sword of this stone and anvil, is rightwise King born of all England.

—Sir Thomas Malory, *Le Morte d'Arthur*

Creative Provinces Can Democratically Create Any Kind of Visionary System to Run Themselves

Creative Provinces are creative democracies: They can democratically create any type of governing social, political, or economic system they want to run themselves, and they can democratically change their system.

We tend to think of democracies based on Greek, Roman, and certain modern models, such as the parliamentary and United States systems. But democratic systems can have just about any shape or form.

Likewise, we have come to think of economic systems in a very limited way, based on such monetary models as capitalism and socialism. We also often forget how vast and important are those parts of our lives that run entirely without money.

And today, as we rely more and more on legal systems, we often forget how important and powerful social systems are in helping us manage human behavior.

With Creative Provinces, however, we can tap our imaginations to create infinitely fun and enchanting ways to manage our human affairs. Provincials can democratically choose to have a Monarchy, a Direct-Democracy Town Meeting system, a Tribal system, a Meritocracy, a Theocracy, a Matriarchy, a Free Enterprise system, a Communal system, a Barter system, a Feudal system, a system of Manners, or almost any other type of social, political, or economic system they can devise, to manage themselves.

Creative Province Visionary Systems Ideally Fit Their Vision

While a Creative Province can democratically adopt any type of governing social, political, or economic system, such a system should fit its Vision. For example:

- A Space Portal Province might democratically choose to be a Representative Meritocracy, run by a Scientific Board consisting of a Chief Astrophysicist, a Chief Mechanical Engineer, a Chief Architect, a Chief Electrical Engineer, a Chief Astronomer, etc.
- A Medieval Province might democratically decide to be run as a Representative Monarchy, with Baronies and such, and also adopt the social system of Chivalry.
- A Victorian Province might run itself entirely by using a system of Victorian Manners, the standard set by the Province's royal family.
- An Indigenous People's Province might embrace its heritage Tribal system.
- A Choral Province might be run by a Choral Master, Keyboard Master, Master Orchestra Conductor, and a Music Committee.
- An Elder Province might work very well combining a representative Council of Elders with a communal sharing of facilities and services.
- An Organic Farm Province might be run like a direct-democracy cooperative.
- An Ancient Egyptian Province could democratically choose to have a rotating Monarchy, with Egyptology students as apprentices, and scholars able to work their way up to the position of Pharaoh.
- A Dog Province might decide to run itself like a neighborhood association, and share a dog park and dog services such as dog training, dog sitting, and grooming.
- A Warrior Province might democratically decide to be a Chiefdom, with a Warrior Chief chosen in an annual battle.
- A Grazing and Hunting Province that held vast open grazing lands and wildernesses might democratically choose to have a Council of Shepherds, Foresters, and Huntsmen run the Province, with a Chief Biologist, a Chief Veterinarian, and Chief Ecologist as advisors.

The possibilities are endless, and more examples are presented in Parts Two and Three of this book.

LIKE ALL DEMOCRACIES, THE CREATIVE PROVINCE SYSTEM MUST BE WELL-STRUCTURED AND WELL-MAINTAINED WITH OATS: OVERSIGHT, ACCOUNTABILITY, TRANSPARENCY, AND SIMPLICITY

In addition to fitting its Vision, to be successful, a Creative Province system must be well structured and well maintained. To successfully accomplish this, the provincial system must have the four foundation pillars of democracy: Oversight, Accountability, Transparency, and Simplicity.

The democratic system must be completely transparent and simple enough so that the member provincials can oversee its activities. Overly large and complex activities are difficult to monitor and can hide corruption.

For example, the structures of globalist multi-national corporations are so large and legally complex that their actions are essentially unknowable and untouchable by "we the people." Thus they can act like modern-day plantations employing modern-day slaves, while hiding behind the disingenuous altruistic wording of "free trade" agreements. And accountability therein is all but nonexistent.

And secret activities are, by their very nature, hiding something—often, unethical behaviors. For example, we see this today in the reported unethical behaviors of many intelligence agencies, whose actions are secret and compartmentalized so that even the people working for them rarely know what their coworkers and chains of command are up to.

Creative Provinces thus need to have OATS to avoid these pitfalls that beset the current globalist world. OATS is further discussed in Part Three.

Wild Geese, Minka/Pixabay

PRINCIPLE 6: CREATIVE PROVINCES ARE FREE AND OPEN WITHIN THEIR PROTECTIVE VISIONARY STRUCTURE

In limitations he first shows himself the master. And the law can only bring us freedom.

—Johann Wolfgang von Goethe,
Was Wir Bringen

Freedom Within Visionary Structure

Creative Provinces adhere to the principle of freedom within their protective visionary structure: They are free and open, both within the Province, and in its relation to the outside world, to all who follow their protective visionary rules. This allows anyone to participate in a Province's creative vision, or to interact with the Province, while at the same time allowing the Province to protect the integrity of its Vision.

Creative Provinces Have Protective Visionary Rules

To protect their Vision in an environment of freedom, all Creative Provinces will establish protective visionary rules, which will include such things as membership requirements, location requirements, and participation requirements. The visionary rules, of course, will need to be within the laws of the sovereign state(s) where the Province physically resides (see Principle 7: Creative Provinces Are in a Complementary Relationship with Sovereign States).

Creative Provinces Are Inclusive Rather Than Exclusive

Creative Provinces are open to anyone who follows their protective visionary rules.

Thus a Creative Province is akin to a community theater: Anyone can participate, but the various roles and other jobs are filled by the participants who are suited to them, and all the activity is done to produce an agreed-upon creative vision. For example:

- A Province of the North Pole might be open to anyone interested in Yule and Christmas and the making and distribution of toys; but it might also have criteria for its Elf Toymakers "to be of diminutive stature and have toymaking skills;" and it might have a system for choosing its Santa Claus among a worldwide network of provincial Santas who are "of large girth with a flowing white beard, and who are accomplished in management and toymaking."

- A Valley Organic Grape Province would be open to anyone to join, but might have a requirement that its vineyards be both organically maintained, and located in its particular valley region.
- A Stream Restoration Province would be open to anyone to join, but might have a requirement that its provincials participate with so many hours of stream-restoration work each month, or some equivalent.
- A Wild West Province would be open to anyone to join, but might have a requirement that its Cowboy provincials be skilled riders and shooters.

PROVINCIALS HAVE THE FREEDOM TO LEAVE OR QUIT A PROVINCE AT ANY TIME

A Creative Province must allow all members the freedom to leave or quit its province at any time. For example:

- A Medieval Province with a feudal system that included "Serfs" would have to allow said Serfs to quit the Province if they wanted to, and not force them to retain their province membership until they worked off some province "debt."
- A Horse Province Road might have numerous connecting properties on which its trail exists. If a provincial with one of these connecting trails wanted to sell their property, the Province would need to make arrangements to somehow keep the trail connection or find an alternate pathway.

Therefore, Creative Provinces will need to establish protective visionary rules so that they are not left "high and dry" should some key provincial suddenly leave.

CREATIVE PROVINCES ARE OPEN TO VISITORS WHO FOLLOW THEIR VISIONARY RULES

Another way Creative Provinces maintain the integrity of their Vision is by requiring visitors to follow their visionary rules. For example:

- A Quiet Province will want to require its visitors to not use radios and other audible devices over a certain decibel level.
- An Addiction Recovery Province might require that visitors not bring in any alcoholic beverages or recreational drugs.
- A Horse Province Road might not allow any motorized vehicles on its trail, with the exception of ambulances and other emergency vehicles.
- An Eighteenth Century Province might require that all guests wear period costume, and might have a collection of wigs, coats, and tri-corn hats available for guests to easily don when visiting, and horses and carriages available for their use.

PROVINCIALS AND VISITORS HAVE THE FREEDOMS OF SPEECH, PRESS, AND ASSEMBLY, AND THE FREEDOM TO ACCESS ANY AND ALL PUBLIC INFORMATION, PROVIDED THEY DO SO BY FOLLOWING THE CREATIVE PROVINCE'S VISIONARY RULES

Provincials and Province visitors must have Humanity's basic freedoms of speech, press, and assembly; but again, these freedoms will be expressed in ways that maintain the Province Vision. For example:

- A Flag Province might be open to anyone who agrees to forgo the use of signs, and instead use flags of various types to advertise their wares, provide directions, and post messages. Visitors would likewise have to remove or cover signs on cars and trucks and replace them with flags.
- A Welsh Province might require its provincials to communicate in Welsh, but in a way that allows its new members time to learn the language.
- A Medieval Province would need to allow its provincial Ladies to speak their minds and practice Wicca, although it might have traditions where under certain circumstances such outspoken ladies would undergo a provincial, kinder, and more fun version of being "burned at the stake."

Provincials must also have access to any and all outside information, providing they do so within the province's visionary rules. For example:

- A Nineteenth Century Province might ensure that its provincials and visitors have access to information via printed news and town criers.
- A World War II Historic and Heritage Culture Province might convey information via its vintage telephones, newspapers, and radio stations.
- News reporters visiting a Natural Light Province might be required to not use flash cameras or other artificial light.
- A researcher requesting information from The Province of Ancient Rome would no doubt receive it in Latin.
- Ancient Alexandria might not allow computers except in a particular wing of its restored Library.

Les Trois Mousquetaires, Joseph-Noël Sylvestré

PRINCIPLE 7: CREATIVE PROVINCES ARE IN A COMPLEMENTARY RELATIONSHIP WITH THEIR SOVEREIGN STATES

The powers not delegated to the United States by the Constitution, nor prohibited by it to the states, are reserved to the states, respectively, or to the people.

Article 10 of the American Bill of Rights[1]

---

1. A Bill of Rights is a "Don't Tread on Me" statement of a citizenry, to ensure its government does not overstep its bounds.

The Two Types of Sovereignty

There are two types of sovereignty: Individual Sovereignty and Group Sovereignty. Of these two, individual sovereignty reigns supreme, as it is given to each person, at birth, by God.

Private property—one's body, abode, and land—is the ultimate expression of individual sovereignty. Thus, the theft or other assault on the body or property, has been decreed unlawful by God in all religious foundations, such as in the Ten Commandments.

Individuals then give further sovereignty to a group, usually a nation-state, *for the purpose of protecting individual sovereignty*, through laws and the administration of justice.

When a person is a part of a group of any type, such as a family, a community such as a creative province, or a sovereign state, they retain their individual sovereignty.

Tyranny happens when people have contrived to steal individual sovereignty via a group. In particular: Tyranny is the takeover of individual sovereignty by the state.

The Relationship between Provincials, Creative Provinces, and the State

Provincials are individuals who have joined together with other individuals who share a community vision. Provincials may be members of one or more Creative Provinces, where they live according to their community Vision. For example, a person might be a provincial member of a Bicycle Province, an Organic Province, and a Wilderness Province, all of which may intersect or overlap at various places.

Provincials also live in and are citizens of Sovereign States, participating in their democratic governments, following their laws, and receiving their protective services. For example, provincials who are members of an Ancient Heritage Province that spans several continents and sovereign states, would also follow the laws of their respective sovereign state governments.

And always, the Individual reigns supreme, owning his or her own life, body, property, and personal vision.

Humanity's Governance: The Sovereign States

There are many individuals and groups that provide services to protect Individual Sovereignty and the Earth. However, it is the Sovereign States that Humanity has given the sovereign power to protect the sovereignty of its States' citizens, through the administration of justice and defense forces.

For example, it is the Sovereign State to which people give the power of arresting and trying people for murder and theft. And it is the Sovereign State to which people give the power of assembling forces for the common defense of their borders from invaders.

To enable this protection, Sovereign States must be stable in their borders, and must administer protective services in a fair and just manner to their varied, heterogeneous populations.

Humanity's Creativity: The Creative Provinces

Creativity comes from the individual human spirit. It can also be manifested through groups where individuals have similar creative visions.

There are many ways in which humans individually and collectively express their creative vision.

Individually, we are all creators of our own life experience and output. We paint pictures, create costumes, cook meals, and plan gatherings.

Collective creativity is expressed through groups of all kinds that share a creative vision: families, shops and businesses, and religious and fraternal organizations.

However, it is intentional communities, and particularly Creative Provinces, which enable complex and inter-harmonious creative community living.

The Complementary Relationship between Sovereign States and Creative Provinces

The Creative Province structure is one in which we can create envisioned communities without having to decide community parameters through our governments.

Our governments can thus be freed from having to deal with the creative visions of their varied populations, and can instead focus on their primary purpose, which is to protect the sovereignty of their individual citizens, through the state's justice system, and by protecting state borders and resources.

The different roles of the sovereign state governments and creative provinces also have the potential of complimenting each other in mutually beneficial ways.

To sovereign states, creative provinces will be able to enhance the state's services and amenities. For example:

- Wilderness Provinces could add buffer zones and connective lands to already existing national protected wilderness parks.
- Environmental Restoration and Preservation Provinces have the potential of significantly assisting with government environmental projects.
- Industry Provinces can empower entrepreneurs, which can help put an end to government programs.
- Transportation and Travelways Provinces have the potential of relieving traffic congestion and other transportation problems that the state must deal with.

In turn, sovereign states provide the aforementioned protective laws and services to provincials; but they also might enhance creative provinces with various kinds of assistance or member lands. For example:

- Several state parks might join a wildlife migration corridor province.
- A state historical park might join a historic province to include its buildings, historic battlefields, and programs in the province.
- A state bicycle trail might join a Bicycle Province Road and expand its reach.

Thus the relationship between Creative Provinces and Sovereign States becomes dynamic and Complementary, as Creative Provinces initiate changes that are beneficial to their outlying communities. More specific examples of this Complementary relationship are presented throughout the rest of this book.

The Structural Weakness of Doing Too Much Under the Umbrella of Government

Many populations have tried to accomplish both governance and creative vision using their sovereign states. But sovereign states, aside from their founding constitutions, are not structured to properly handle creative vision. The sovereign state must be free to work on its main mission: to administer protective services to its many and varied citizens.

A Suppression and Oppression of Individual Sovereignty and Community Creativity

Sovereign States should not be in the role of manifesting creative lifestyles—for example, a particular religion, a particular type of landscaping, or a particular health regime. If it does, then one of two things happen:

To be fair to its varied population, those lifestyle choices have to be watered down with all sorts of compromises, in order to "make everyone happy." That is the ultimate suppression of creativity. Or,

If a Sovereign State tries to establish a creative lifestyle that is not watered down, but is what its citizens with the most influence want, it ends up imposing it on people who don't want it, or removing people who refuse to go along with it, with oppressive results.

WEAKENED SOVEREIGN GOVERNMENTS

Our small, local communities have been increasingly "weakened by expansion" caused by the advent of the Industrial Age, particularly vehicles on land, sea, and air—the primary methods for expanding individual spheres of influence.

To deal with this weakening of local communities, humanity has increasingly looked to the sovereign state to pick up the slack. Thus we move from private, locally based programs to assist people who need help, to large government programs; we move from small neighborhood or village schools, to large, state-run schools; and we move from individually chosen health regimes, to state mandated health regimes. Indeed it seems there is hardly any aspect of our lives that today is not controlled to some extent by some law or government program.

Of course, government safety nets can be an important aspect of the sovereign state's protective role. But now these governments have, as a result of too much reliance on them, gotten way too big.

So today we have this situation of Humanity attempting to function way too much through its governments. The overburdened sovereign state then becomes too large, and its plethora of hidden passageways becomes more and more susceptible to hiding corruption. And when a government becomes corrupt, its citizenry loses control of it.

A Dynamic, and Complementary Relationship

But we can amend our current situation of trying to handle too much of Humanity's affairs under the aegis of the Sovereign State, by going back to working within our local communities, especially Creative Provinces.

Creative Provinces will exist under the protective umbrella of Sovereign States, which will utilize Creative Provinces to compliment their services and amenities. A dynamic and Complementary relationship will thus develop between Creative Provinces and Sovereign States.

Mt. Eaton Wayne Co. Ohio Barn Raising with men working on roof behind oak shocks,
© Doyle Yoder Photography

Principle 8: Creative Provinces Hold to the Highest Principles of Creating Community Life as a Magnificent, Beautiful, and Loving Art Form

I saw the angel in the marble and carved until I set him free.

—Michelangelo

Resolving the Octave: Life As Art

In Principle Eight we resolve the octave of the eight principles of Creative Provinces. As such, Principle Eight is the higher octave of Principle One.

In Principle One we envision the angel in the marble, and in Principle Eight we carve it until we set him free. We develop our Vision until it becomes a work of art.

Creative Provinces are Life as Art: We manifest our lives, individually and as a community, as works of art. We help each other to create together. And this is not just any creation we can come up with. With Creative Provinces we create and live the most magnificent, beautiful, and loving visions we desire.

And this requires of us a change in our approach to living.

Creating what we want requires a change of attitude and resonance.

In order to create what we want, we must change our attitude and our resonance. This requires that we move away from any negative mindset that says "life is hard" and that it must be filled with drudgery, strife, torture, poverty, confinement, ugliness, riots, and violence. Such mindsets and activities are the ultimate in trying to get what we want by doing things "the hard way." When we constantly watch, think about, and participate in these negative activities, we resonate with their vibrations and contribute to manifesting them.

Instead, we must change our thinking to become Life Artists: Here we see that we are creative beings, living in a great, magnificent creation. We were created in the image of the Prime Creator; indeed, we are children of, and aspects of, that great Creator, who gave us free will. As such, we have the power to create magnificent realities. When we resonate with the divine creation, we see that we can manifest the beautiful lives we have always wanted.

Art Evolved to Life

In Creative Provinces we evolve art to *the lives we live.*

The First Dimension of Art

In the *first* dimension of art, we make individual creations, for ourselves, and to share: We paint pictures; we make sculptures; we take photographs; we write stories; we make music—play an instrument or compose or sing a song; we make clothing, gardens, crafts; we prepare food; and so on.

The Second Dimension of Art

In the *second* dimension of art, we make more complex creations with others: We make elaborate films; we compose or perform in orchestral works and choruses; we write and put on plays; we put together religious services; we illustrate and publish books; we build automobiles and cathedrals; we hold dances; we create restaurants and hold feasts; we create historical reenactments; and we create other elaborate events such as weddings and festivals. All of these group creations use aspects of the first dimension of art.

The Third Dimension of Art

In the *third* dimension of art, *we create our entire lives as works of art, and help others create a community with us*: We create and live in beautiful, enchanting communities; we travel on magnificent byways; and we work doing the things we love. All of these artistically created communities, byways, and industries use aspects of the first two dimensions of art.

How Creative Provinces Live Artistically

There are many things that can help people create provinces and live artistically. Aside from the ideas and guidance provided in Parts 2 and 3 of this book, the following are some basic things to consider:

Improving on and Embellishing the Past

With Creative Provinces we have the opportunity to take our Heritage and improve upon it.

Our history is everywhere filled with wars, injustices, and tortures. These were part of Humanity's learning process. But these were also creations that shaped us, and gave our history its excitement, and gave our art its pathos and drama.

When we recreate our historical cultures, then, we have the opportunity to remove their violence and injustices, and honor our forebears who endured these hardships, while at the same time capturing their excitement and beauty. Thus in Creative Provinces:

- We can revive dueling, skirmishes, and warfare in friendly, provincial ways, using less dangerous methods of combat;
- We can replace the slavery, serfdom, and other physical and economic confinements that existed in most historical societies, with egalitarian roles and opportunities;
- And we can replace the burnings, scalpings, beheadings, and tortures with kind, enlightened, and fun activities.

With Creative Provinces we also have the opportunity to embellish our Heritage cultures with monumental beauty and enchantment that everyone—not just a small class of people—has access to; and we can give everyone opportunities to take special roles—everything from Pharaoh to Santa Claus. Such an approach to our past allows us to recreate these cultures in their ideal, magnificent forms.

Artists Show Us How to Live Life as Art

We are blessed with countless artists—painters, filmmakers, writers, chefs, costume designers, architects, and more—who are showing us how to manifest our lives as works of art. *They are showing us how to live!*

Of course, artists also show us all manner of horrors, murders, dystopias, and other evils. These are also important aspects of art, as they show us how to keep such evils at bay in order to live the magnificent lives we desire.

LIVING EXAMPLES OF LIFE AS ART

There are currently many Intentional Communities that live Life as Art: Eco-villages have created havens that produce food sustainably and protect the environment. Religious communities have created places that live the religious life of devotion, prayer, meditation, and peaceful activities. And retirement communities have created places where elders share activities and assistance.

All of these intentional communities have a vision by which they live. Some of these visions include fashion, such as the habits and robes of the religious; some include food production; some include services.

Of the many current intentional communities, the most long-lived and successful is the one with a structure closest to that of the Creative Province: The Amish.

The Amish have created a full way of life, with everything from their style, their religion, their language, and their philosophy, to their industry and their travel. And they have successfully maintained their creation over several centuries, with protective rules that keep out cultural invaders.

DOING THINGS BEAUTIFULLY

> *"La bella figura...it's at the heart of Italian life... it's about doing things beautifully."*
> —Alexander McCall Smith, *My Italian Bulldozer*

One of the best examples of "doing things beautifully" is the Amish barn-raising: Not only is the finished barn a thing of beauty, so is *the process* of building the barn. The people arrive by horse and buggy; they are dressed in beautifully designed homespun Amish clothing. The men are building with local wood they have milled themselves and they use their own often hand-hewn tools. The women have brought a delicious meal made from scratch in their own kitchens, from foods grown in their own gardens with care for both the soil and the wildlife, which are integral to their growth. The horses are treated respectfully and participate in the work.

There are no products made in sweat shops or factory farms; there are no pesticides poisoning the land, wildlife, and food.

That sort of ugliness is unnecessary, and indeed *has never been necessary*. It was all an experiment that has shown us how we do not want to live.

There are so many ways we can do things beautifully, to make our lives "works of art." We can dress for dinner and other occasions, and we can add flowers to our surroundings. We can observe cultural niceties, and speak with courtesy. We can use the beautiful objects we have inherited.

We can take the slow, back roads on our journeys, and stop to greet people in friendship. We can help the animals in our care to have joyous and purposeful lives. We can give even the smallest of gifts to others to show that we care about them.

And now we can embrace the beauty, magnificence, and love that we have always wanted for everyone, everywhere, by creating the enchanting communities of our fondest dreams.

A Review of the Octave

Earth's Eight Solar "Royal" Cardinal Points, a coloration by the author, of a mandala drawn by Alberta Hutchinson.

Let us now review the octave, depicted above as a mandala, to see how Creative Provinces develop:

In Principle One we declare our Vision, with ourselves and our properties, and connect with others with the same Vision.

In Principle Two, we make our Vision Real, with real people, places, and activities.

In Principle Three we stretch, grow, and take shape as a physical community, as we add individuals and properties.

In Principle Four we create, appreciate, revive, maintain, protect, and use our Heritage Treasures.

In Principle Five we create a visionary-appropriate way to run ourselves.

In Principle Six we give ourselves and others, visionary-appropriate ways to interact with us.

In Principle Seven we live in a Complementary relationship with our sovereign state.

And in Principle Eight, the Vision we declared in Principle One is now fully manifested as we commit to creating this provincial community as a magnificent, beautiful, and loving art form.

PART 2

THE FOUR TYPES OF CREATIVE PROVINCES, WITH EXAMPLES

Transportation and Travelways Provinces / *65*

Industry Provinces / *89*

Environment Provinces / *112*

Cultural Provinces / *134*

Introduction to Part 2

The Four Basic Types of Creative Provinces

There are four main types of Creative Provinces: Transportation and Travelway, Industry, Environment, and Cultural. Every Creative Province will be founded on one Primary Vision, and for ease of categorization, the Province's Primary Vision will indicate its main Province Type. But Creative Provinces will also have Supporting Visions, often including all of these four types of endeavors.

For example, an Organic Small-Farm Province would probably want to classify itself as an Industry Province, and wording to the effect of "A creative province of small, organic farms that market cooperatively" might be its driving, Primary Vision. But that Province would also want to protect and enhance its many environmental treasures, such as the integrity of its land, water, and air resources; it might gradually include provincial travelways, such as horse roads; and it might gradually develop a provincial culture, to include such activities as harvest balls and barn raisings. These visions would be included among the Province's Supporting Visions.

Thus, even though they are categorized in one main category, Creative Provinces will nevertheless want to advertise themselves according to all of their important Visions. For example, a Medieval Province might be categorized mainly as a Cultural Province, but might also advertise itself as a horse province and a sheep-herding province.

To demonstrate the different types of Creative Provinces and Visions, I have made up examples throughout the book, and given them names and descriptions. Some of these examples are very practical and might be relatively easy to manifest, others are very ambitious, and a few are downright whimsical!

I. Transportation and Travelways Provinces

Cattle Drive, iStock.com/Life Journeys

While all Creative Provinces will have transportation—travelways to them and within them, and one or more particular modes of transportation—some will be created with the Primary Vision of manifesting a certain mode of transportation, or to make a unique travelway to connect two or more creative provinces or non-province areas.

Thus we define Transportation and Travelways Provinces as follows:

> ***Transportation Provinces*** *are Creative Provinces that feature a certain type of transportation as their primary vision, and* ***Travelways Provinces*** *are Creative Provinces that are travelways with the primary vision of being devoted to a certain type of travel for humans and/or other creatures.*

Thus, Transportation Provinces might be such things as walk neighborhoods, bicycle cities, golf-cart islands, trolley-car towns, and horse communities.

And Travelways Provinces might be such things as pedestrian trails, bicycle roads, horse roads, historic train lines, hot-air balloon corridors, wildlife migration corridors, or open-range cattle drive routes.

Creative Provinces thus present us with an opportunity to be creative in our transportation so that we are not overwhelmed by any one method—as has happened, for example, with motor vehicles. In our enthusiasm for those wonderful inventions, we have allowed them to crowd-out all manner of other types of wonderful ground transport: horses and horse-drawn vehicles, elephants, camels, skis, trains and trolleys, bicycles and other pedaled vehicles, and an endless variety of other modes of travel, including all manner of human and animal pedestrians. A similar situation exists with water and air travel.

But fortunately there is an answer: People can create transportation and travelways provinces suitable to their population, climate, natural resources, terrain, and creative vision.

As described in Principle Eight, with our creative transportation and travelways we can include travel in our quest to become Life Artists. Instead of always hurrying up to take the fastest and most convenient way to a destination, we can include travel and transportation as part of our creative experience. Thus:

We can enjoy the experience of walking a fairy-lit woodland footpath on an evening visit to our neighbor;

We can paddle a canoe down a stream to visit our friends;

We can take our horse and wagon to the local farmer's market;

We can sail on a vintage ocean liner, complete with period dress and activities, as part of our vacation overseas;

We can arrive at a Roman bath in a chariot;

We can bicycle on a scenic route to attend a meeting;

We can ski over mountain trails to attend church in the next village;

And we can enjoy a sleigh ride over the hills and through the woods as part of the wonderful experience of visiting grandmother.

Here is our opportunity to embrace beauty, adventure, and magic in our journeys through life.

ANIMAL TRANSPORTATION AND TRAVELWAYS PROVINCES

The Road, Winter, Otto Knirsch, 1853,
Currier & Ives lithograph with hand coloring

I think that of all the types of Transportation and Travelways Provinces imaginable, Animal Transportation and Travelways Provinces are the most wonderful, because they are filled with Life.

Animal Transportation and Travelways Provinces will be places where motorized or other mechanical vehicles will be either limited in some way, or abandoned altogether in favor of transport animals, or they will be places designated as migration corridors for wildlife, or routes for livestock.

Domestic animals such as horses, and their close cousins, burrows, mules, donkeys, and camels, will be particularly suited to such creative provinces. But other domestic creatures might also be featured in transportation, such as in elephant, goat-cart, and dogsled provinces. In some provinces, homing pigeons (the "Racing Homer") might be used to carry messages.

We might also go beyond these traditional transport animals. As Humanity becomes more sophisticated with genetic engineering, we might bring back certain species, such as pterodactyls, which might be the starting point for genetically creating large domesticated avian creatures to carry people through the sky.

A Note on Categorization: Although transport animals are "working animals," we are separating this type of Creative Province from the later-described "Working Animal Provinces," which are "Industry Provinces" that feature animals working at any number of jobs, and "Featured Animal Provinces," which are environments that feature and protect a certain animal. The difference is in the Primary Vision. For example, a "Cowboy Province," which included cattle ranches, a beef industry, and a cowboy culture, would probably classify itself as an Industry Province. But those provincials might also form Cattle Drive Routes for driving their cattle to area markets, which they would classify as a Travelways Province. And there may be a creative province that protects free-ranging wild mustangs, which would be classified as a Featured Animal Province.

In addition to domestic animals, wild creatures will feature prominently in travelways provinces, particularly as a way to preserve wildlife migration corridors.

Example: Currier & Ives Horse Province

Horse Provinces can be formed in areas of all kinds of population densities, from rural countrysides to urban neighborhoods. In cities, local breweries might want to deliver their beer kegs to neighboring pubs using beloved draft horses, such as the Shire and Percheron, pulling drays; equestrians might add horse trails to their local parks; and history re-creators can bring back horse-drawn carriages. All it takes are people joining in, to make their properties and areas horse-friendly.

In this example, a Currier & Ives Horse Province is formed in a northern rural area, with the Vision of gradually shifting to using horses for year-round transportation throughout the Province. Provincials gradually convert their garages and lots to stables and corrals. In Province areas where houses aren't built with enough land to keep horses, provincials create shared pastures and stables. Provincials also gradually establish commercial stables with horses, cabs, and carriages for hire. Snow removal is scaled down to favor horse-drawn sleighs. Currier & Ives-inspired art becomes a significant feature of the Province culture.

| EXAMPLE: COUNTRYSIDE HORSE ROAD

A Horse Road Province is a road linking two or more Horse Provinces or non-province areas, and which limits motorized and other mechanical transportation, to enable traveling by horse to a destination.

In this example, people in a rural area encompassing several villages, form a Countryside Horse Road. Provincials begin by linking their properties to make sections of the road, which connect the villages and many outlying farms and other properties.

Over time, as the Countryside Horse Road develops, provincials establish inns with stables, cobblers, tack shops, and other horse-friendly accommodations, along the routes.

| EXAMPLE: QUEEN OF SHEBA CAMEL CARAVAN TRADE ROUTE

The romance of the Middle East is embodied in the culture of the Camel. There is nothing quite as mysterious and majestic as the camel caravan, the train of these stately giants gliding like ships through its vast deserts, ridden by travelers fully cloaked against the incessant waves of heat and sand.

In this example, people form a Queen of Sheba Camel Caravan Trade Route, reviving the ancient road that stretched northward from Mareb, along eastern Arabia, and on to Gaza. Mareb was the Tenth Century B.C. center of the frankincense and myrrh trade, at the time called "the land of the two paradises," because of its rich farms that flanked either side of the Dhana River. During the reign of the Queen of Sheba, Mareb was the greatest city of the Arabian Peninsula.

On this province road, motorized vehicles are restricted to emergency vehicles. Provincials establish oases along the road, along with other amenities for camels and their riders.

The Queen of Sheba Camel Caravan Trade Route eventually connects many ancient Middle Eastern and Mediterranean Historic and Heritage Culture Provinces.

Example: Trumpeter Swan Migration Corridor

To help protect the migration routes of wildlife, people can form migration corridor provinces encompassing the areas where various forms of wildlife migrate.

Currently there are proto-provinces of this type, such as the Jaguar Corridor, an initiative created by *Panthera*, which works with governments, companies, and land owners to create protected swaths of land where the big cat can live and travel;[1] and the Monarch Joint Venture,[2] which has linked up many organizations with Monarch Butterfly preservation programs, and has resources to help individuals create Monarch habitats.

In our example, people form a Trumpeter Swan Migration Corridor Province to protect the routes of this exquisite bird. Provincials provide wetlands and nesting islands and fields along the route, and help to remove impediments to their travel.

This creative province forms a federation with the Swan Lakes Province (described in the Featured Animal Province section). It might also team up with such organizations as the Trumpeter Swan Society,[3] which assists with swan migration. The result is a magnificent marshland corridor whose member provincials are magically visited twice yearly by their namesakes.

---

1. Panthera is a wildcat conservation organization founded in 2006. From "The Jaguar Freeway," Sharon Guynup, *Smithsonian*, October 2011.
2. Monarchjointventure.org
3. TrumpeterSwanSociety.org

PEDESTRIAN TRANSPORTATION AND TRAVELWAYS PROVINCES

Winter Landscape with Skaters, Adriaen van de Venne

Pedestrian Transportation & Travelways Provinces are those that feature various kinds of human-powered transportation, particularly walking, bicycling, skiing, and skating.

In such creative provinces people will use these pedestrian modes for transportation, rather than just for recreation (which has been the trend since the overwhelming use of the automobile).

EXAMPLE: NORTH COUNTRY SKI PROVINCE

Skis were initially used for pedestrian travel during winter. Once again, using skis for travel has been mostly abandoned in favor of the automobile, but it can be revived by forming Province Ski Travelways.

In this example, a North Country Ski Province is started in an area that includes several downhill ski resorts and many cross-country ski trails. The Province Vision is to connect the resorts and nearby villages with a network of cross-country ski trails, and to convert certain snowplowed roads to non-plowed roads, for travel by ski and sleigh.

The Province allows motorized sleds on its roads at certain times, which is especially helpful for breaking paths after a heavy snowfall, and it reserves other times exclusively for pedestrian skiing and horse-drawn sleighs.

Example: Cross-Congo Aerial Way

Aerial Walkways can be an enchanting way of traveling between places, particularly in areas where there is a need to be above ground, such as over streets and highways, rivers, rugged mountain passes, and wildernesses. Examples include the Banff Wildlife Crossings in Alberta, Canada, which provide safe passage for wildlife of all kinds over the Trans-Canada Highway, and Peru's Rope Bridges, such as the one that hangs over the Pampas River.

In this example, a Cross-Congo Aerial Way is formed to create a network of aerial travelways through the African Congo Jungle. The Province travelway develops into a vast network of aerial walkways, beginning with Rwanda's Nyungwe National Park Canopy Walkway, and extending through other parts of the Congo rainforest, adding more high tech walkways, as well as rustic aerial walkways and swinging vines.

The Cross-Congo Aerial Way becomes a major addition to wildlife tourism in the Congo, and as it grows, provincials build and connect tree-house inns and cafés, and similar amenities, eventually creating a magnificent travelway unparalleled in its wild beauty.

Example: Good Neighbors Walk Province

We've all delighted in quaint "walk streets" where you feel like you've stepped back in time to a quieter, neighbor-friendly age. Some of these walk streets are shopping streets that are closed off to motor traffic, such as in Santa Monica, California. Others are residential neighborhoods where designated streets are closed to motor vehicles, such as in nearby Venice, California.

But why stop with just a few streets? Whole cities, such as Venice, Italy, and islands, such as Mackinaw Island in Michigan, show us some of the magical possibilities of replacing motor transportation with alternative travel.

In this example, people in a residential area form a Good Neighbors Walk Province. The residential area already has a few long-standing walk streets, from which the Province expands. Most nearby residential blocks have both a front horizontal street and back alley, making it possible for more streets to be closed to motor vehicles, with the alleys and vertical cross streets remaining open to them.

Soon this Province grows to a much-enlarged area from that of the few original walk streets, and the municipal government eventually gets on board, assisting with redirecting vehicular traffic.

Example: Sunrise Bicycle Province and Great Sunrise Bicycle Road

Today there are many bicycle paths in and around most cities and regions, and organizations and governments at all levels have done wonderful work creating and maintaining them. But still there are usually too few bicycle paths, and they are often too inconveniently placed, or they dangerously share the road with motor vehicles, for people to want to use them as a significant mode of travel. And usually there just aren't enough funds for communities to greatly expand their bicycle paths.

But such existing paths *can* be greatly expanded upon by creating Bicycle Province Travelways.

In addition to Bicycle Province Roads, Bicycle Provinces, where travel within the province is by bicycle, can be created in appropriate regions, such as those that are relatively flat and have a temperate climate.

In this dual example, a Sunrise Bicycle Province is started in a metropolitan area with an already sizeable number of bicyclists. The Province Vision is to accumulate an increasing number of streets to be used exclusively for peddled vehicles and pedestrians. The Province establishes parking areas for motor vehicles in convenient locations, where people can exchange their cars for bicycles.

As the Province grows, a provincial bicycle industry and a bicycle culture develop.

From its metropolitan starting point, a Great Sunrise Bicycle Road begins, extending from the Sunrise Bicycle Province to outlying areas. This Province has a large vision: to expand across the continent, connecting one town and city to another with bicycle roads. In some places, the Great Sunrise Bicycle Road is devoted exclusively to bicycles and pedestrians; in other places it shares the road with animal pedestrians, particularly horses and elephants.

Motor Vehicle Transportation and Travelways Provinces

InDesign GenAi Assets

Cars are probably the most wonderful invention of the Twentieth Century, giving us the incredible freedom to travel great distances, where and when we will. But we can actually have much more fun with them, while at the same time giving ourselves ways to not be excessive with them. We can do this by creating Motor Vehicle Transportation and Travelways Provinces—places where motorized vehicle travel is totally different from what is the norm today.

Provinces can be created that feature a particular type of motor vehicle. The possibilities are endless: Vintage cars, neon-colored electric cars, racecars, steam-powered vehicles. The vehicles can be small, tiny, relatively slow, unusual looking, oddly shaped, amphibious, non-combustion, solar powered, trash-powered, brightly colored, all colored the same, or made of unlikely materials.

Many motor-vehicle proto-provinces already exist, such as Cave Creek, Arizona, a community that draws motorcyclists. The desert climate and terrain are conducive to motorcycling, and the Wild West motif and cowboy culture are a magnet for motor-

revved-up testosterone and men tough as rawhide. Lest you think such a place might be devoid of other culture, I must add that Cave Creek is also a bustling artist community, appealing to Western artists with styles ranging from aboriginal to contemporary.

Another motor vehicle proto-province is Bermuda, where visitor transportation is by moped.

In the provincial world, automobile manufacturers will become smaller, more numerous, more localized, and more specialized, as they cater to provincials with orders for specialized vehicles.

Example: Great Gatsby Antique Automobile Province

Travel by antique and vintage automobiles of a particular period, or their reproductions, can be the defining Vision of a Transportation Province or Province Travelway.

In this example, a Great Gatsby Antique Automobile Province is started by the members of two antique car clubs who live in and around a quaint seaside village, which also has many houses built in the 1920s, and in a nearby city with several neighborhoods built in the 1920s.

The Province begins with encouraging travel by antique car within its domain, and over time it draws more people with cars of the 1920s, as well as amenities and services, such as antique car repair, and a vintage car reproduction industry.

The Great Gatsby Antique Automobile Province eventually develops into a full Heritage Province. See this description in the Cultural Provinces section.

Example: Lightning Bolt Electric Car Province

In this example, people form a Lightning Bolt Electric Car Province, with the Vision of an extensive network of roads and facilities where electric cars can be easily purchased, rented, recharged, and serviced.

The Province keeps an extensive and current map that shows its roads, for ease of travel. Electric car owners and renters join the Lightning Bolt Province and help to keep its extensive network current.

Example: Steam Engine Province

The Stanley Steamer was one of the most successful of the early steam-engine vehicles. It could run on almost anything that could burn. Drivers could pick up sticks from the roadside and throw them into the burner. Farmers with steam-powered tractors could power them with their own farm waste.

In this example, industrious people start a Steam Engine Province, where steam-engine vehicles are revived, developed, and driven: cars, tractors, and other vehicles of all sizes and shapes, and made of, and steam-powered by, all manner of materials.

Provincials take into account safety and pollution control, but certain allowances are made for experimentation. One feature of the provincial culture is that the men wear handlebar mustaches.

Example: Crocodile Solar Cart Province

There are already numerous small communities that use golf carts for traveling about. These small, quiet vehicles are ideal for wildlife-preservation areas, senior communities, and other areas where short-distance, leisurely travel and natural quietude are desired.

In this example, a Crocodile Solar Cart Province is formed in a region in and around an extensive wetlands preservation park, with a Vision to use small, solar-powered, and wildlife-friendly vehicles as its primary form of non-pedestrian transportation. The Province also takes steps to ensure that its solar-powered vehicles have certain wildlife safety features, such as crocodile leg-guards, and backup electric batteries so that you can escape if your solar battery runs out right when the crocodile is about to chomp on your leg.

The Province draws to it, solar cart manufacturers, rentals, sales, and services. It also develops a provincial culture that features the crocodile.

RAIL TRANSPORTATION AND TRAVELWAYS PROVINCES

The Dixie Flagler, © by Betty Ann Fraley

Rail Transportation Provinces are creative provinces that have as either their primary vision or a supporting vision, transportation *within* their province by tracked vehicle. San Francisco, California; New Orleans, Louisiana; Melkmarket, Antwerp; and Alfana, Lisbon are all examples of proto-provinces of this type.

Rail Travelways Provinces are provincial train lines that extend between creative provinces or non-province areas.

Every existing train and train line, as well as streetcars, subways, trolleys, and other tracked vehicles have the potential of being used to create unique, Rail Provinces. People can work with existing lines so that these trains can become provincial and marvelously unique, and people can rebuild or create new rail lines.

There are interesting train lines throughout the world, many of which combine travel with sightseeing and specialty dining. The Society of International Railway Travelers lists many of these, including the famous Orient Express. Such train lines can be excellent starting places for provincial development.

There is no limit to the provincial characteristics rail provinces can have. Historic Train Lines can provide period travel between Nineteenth and Twentieth Century Historic and Heritage Provinces. Other trains can house universities, libraries, the performing arts, a particular cuisine, or an activity.

Example: Lincoln-Davis Train Line

Heritage train lines can be run between Historic and Heritage Culture Provinces, as well as non-province areas. On such province train lines people would follow the customs of the period. For example, an Edwardian Train Line would feature Edwardian period costume and other markers of that culture.

In this example, a Lincoln-Davis Province Train Line is formed as a train line dedicated to the American Civil War period. It becomes an integral transportation connection between many Nineteenth Century Provinces, with additional stops in non-province places. Battle re-enactors and other provincials use the train, as do others who are willing to conform to the dress and customs of the period.

Example: The Sugar Train

The Sugar Train on the Hawaiian island of Maui is a quaint ride into the past. It travels through a sugar plantation, while musicians serenade with mandolin, and travelers sip coconut milk.

In our example, a Sugar Train Province is created beginning with just such a train. The train is expanded from a tourist attraction to be reinstated as a train line for travel. As the Sugar Train Province expands, it becomes a major feature of a larger, Rustic Hawaii Province, which includes the revival of Hawaii's heritage industries, heritage culture, and the restoration of its heritage rustic environment.

See more descriptions of Rustic Hawaii in the Cultural Provinces section.

Example: The Soul Train

In this example, a Soul Train is started as a train line connecting various African-American Historic and Heritage Culture Provinces including a Harlem Heritage Province, a

Province of Motown, and a Brer Rabbit Heritage Province. The Primary Vision of the Soul Train is to connect to various creative provinces, as well as non-province areas, and to feature soul food and entertainment.

The Soul Train features the music and cuisine of African-American heritage culture, as well as discussion groups and readings, and it houses a library. It eventually becomes a segment of a larger Train of Thought Province, described below.

Example: The Train of Thought

In this example, a Train of Thought is created as a province train line that meanders around the world, connecting creative provinces as well as non-province areas, with the primary vision of a devotion to intellectual and creative discussion, performance, and study. Its trains become veritable libraries of interesting books, with salons, discussion parlors, readings, workshops, and cafés.

As the Train of Thought grows, it eventually includes in its provincial network, a number of small province train lines that specialize in a particular type of study or creative endeavor: A Ghandi-Tagore Train Line; a Jane Austen Train Line; a Sartre-Beauvoir Existentialist Train Line; an Impressionist Painting Train Line; a Soul Train; and an Unsolved Mysteries Train Line.

AIR TRANSPORTATION AND TRAVELWAYS PROVINCES

Steampunk, Artie NaVarre/Pixabay

As with the automobile on land, in our air spaces we have inadvertently created a "global jet plane province." While the airplane is a great invention, we must make room for all manner of other wonderful and magical types of air travel. With Creative Provinces, we can do just that: we can be enormously creative with our air transportation.

Creative Provinces specializing in hot air balloons, Zeppelins, experimental aircraft, spacecraft, period airplanes, gliders, live airborne transport creatures, and aircraft of all manner of shapes and sizes, are just some of the interesting and fun possibilities for provincial airways.

> *Example: Rainbow Balloon Province and Balloon Corridor*
>
> Hot Air Balloon Provinces are among the most exciting and enchanting creative provinces I can think of. Imagine: regions where hot-air balloons are a primary mode of transportation between distant points!
>
> In this example, hot-air balloon enthusiasts form a Rainbow Balloon Province and Balloon Corridor, a creative province of people dedicated to hot-air ballooning. The Province has many provincials who live in far-flung places,

but there are also some closely grouped provincial properties, enabling Province hubs to form.

Thus the Province forms a network of hot-air balloon airstream pathways among and between these hubs, and also forms some pathways that are fairly reliable for hot-air balloon travel between more distant points. With its Rainbow Balloon Corridor, the Province is thus able to connect many areas where provincials have created enchanting enclaves.

As the Province develops, it creates a network of Balloon Corridors and Balloon Ports, as it adds the many properties of provincials along desired routes, providing additional balloon landing areas, and ballooning services and amenities.

The Province develops an industry of making and servicing hot-air balloons, hosting Hot Air Balloon Festivals, and giving balloon rides and transportation to adventurous souls. A provincial ballooning culture emerges, making this Province one of the most enchanting and colorful places to live.

Example: Red Baron Province

Historic Airplane Provinces will specialize in a particular era of airplanes, such as the early experimental aircraft of the Wright Brothers at Kitty Hawk, or World War II-era planes.

In this example, a Red Baron Province, named after famed German Ace, Manfred von Richthofen, is created for the revival of World War I-era planes for travel and reenactments. Both restored and recreated Caudrons, Breguets, Morane-Saulniers, Capronis, Sikorskys, Sopwiths, Curtisses, and many more of the 223 plane models employed during the war are used by the Province, with many new aces added to the rolls.

The Red Baron Province becomes affiliated with various early-Twentieth Century provinces, and its planes become an integral form of transportation between them.

Example: Star Trek Space Portal Province

Space Portal Provinces might form in and around existing government or private space centers, in order to expand on the facility, both culturally and in terms of its intellectual reach. Already there are proto-provinces around such government facilities, as private companies locate nearby to provide services for government contracts and their many offshoots.

In this example, people form a Star Trek Space Portal Province in and around an existing government space center. The Province specializes in research, industries, services, and cultural activities that support space travel.

The Star Trek Space Portal Province eventually combines with an Other Worlds Space City (see the example in the Artistic and Architectural Concept Provinces section), and other similar creative provinces, to form an Earth-Space Portal Province Federation.

Example: Sky King Province

People who live in remote and sparsely populated areas where travel by small plane is often necessary, can certainly benefit by forming Small Plane Provinces.

In this example, a Sky King Province is formed (taking its name from the vintage television drama) in a remote wilderness area. The Province Vision is to accumulate and coordinate small aircraft services in its vast region.

Sky King provincials create and share landing fields on their properties, and coordinate services, such as mechanical repairs, and amenities, such as field lunches, maps, and overnight accommodations. The Province also develops a viable provincial industry of wilderness searches.

WATER TRANSPORTATION AND TRAVELWAYS PROVINCES

The Mississippi in Time of Peace, Frances Flora Bond Palmer, 1865, Currier & Ives lithograph

Travel by stream, river, and seaway has been vastly reduced in modern times, and in many places totally forgotten, once again due to the dominant culture of the automobile. The ubiquitous network of automobile roads, bridges, and tunnels has made it much easier to travel by land than by waterway. In addition, dams in streams (mostly unused today) interrupt such travel—not to mention interrupt aquatic-life migration. Airplane travel has had a similar effect on water travel. And as they have been increasingly forgotten as travelways, these bodies of water, which once figured so prominently in local culture, are also forgotten in many other ways, and are barely registered in consciousness as people drive over bridges, through tunnels, and fly high overhead.

In Humanity's quest for technological convenience and ease, it has once again shoved aside a beautiful, exciting, fun, and exhilarating way of traveling. But by provincializing, people can reclaim their waterways for travel.

Thus streams, canals, rivers, lakes, seas, and oceans will form the basis of Water Transportation and Travelways Provinces. Many of these waterways will also be integral elements of Historic and Heritage Culture Provinces, beginning with the restoration, reproduction, and reinstatement of historic ships and other watercraft. Other Cultural Provinces will find excitement in creating new watercraft. Other waterways will figure prominently in Environment and Industry Provinces. For example, a Willow Creek Province (described in the Environment Provinces section) would envision reclaiming a local stream for travel.

EXAMPLE: MISSISSIPPI RIVER HERITAGE PROVINCE

In this example, a Mississippi River Heritage Province is begun by people with properties and businesses in historic river ports and other key properties along the Mississippi, and by people who own and operate historic riverboats and other river-centered heritage industries.

The Province Vision is to restore, recreate, and reinstate historic ports and boats of all types on the river, and to use these for significant travel.

Gradually, more properties and watercraft are added to the Province, so that eventually they operate over lengthy sections of the river, with numerous stops at historic and period boatyards and boat launches.

The Mississippi River Heritage Province eventually teams up with numerous Historic and Heritage Culture Provinces along the river, all of which will want to include period river travel as an integral part of their Province. Eventually large swaths of the Mississippi are devoted to travel via period riverboats.

EXAMPLE: PLEIN AIR CANAL PROVINCE

In this example, a Plein Air Canal Province is formed in an area with historic canals, where people want to expand on the concept. The Primary Vision is to gradually expand on the original canals with canal tributaries to nearby neighborhoods and other areas for local travel by watercraft, and to create a quiet and beautiful place that will encourage *plein air* (French for "out in the open air") artists.

The Province draws to it, small boat-building and boat-rental industries, and many canal-side launches, cafés, shops, and other businesses.

The plein air artists, who paint along the banks, are drawn to the Province's quiet beauty and the portraiture clientele from the canal's many shops and cafés.

Example: The Chao Phraya River Province

In this example, people create a Chao Phraya River Province with the Vision of preserving travel along Thailand's rivers and klongs using traditional long tail boats. Another vision of the Province is to preserve and encourage the historic river architecture, such as the wooden houses built on stilts that line some of the river's shores. The Province soon expands to protect and enhance other cultural treasures of the Chao Phraya, as well as the river's ecology.

Example: Heritage Lighthouse and Sea Lanes Province

In this example, a Heritage Lighthouse and Sea Lanes Province is formed along a coastal region where provincial ocean-going ships and boats come to port. The Primary Vision of the Province is to restore the usage of heritage lighthouses, and use them to assist in the heritage navigation of traditional ships—passenger, freight, and fishing. The Province also uses other traditional communications and navigation equipment, and assists in other ways, provincial travel along the coast and sea-lanes.

The Heritage Lighthouse and Sea Lanes Province teams up with creative provinces that use tall ships and other heritage boats and ships, as well as with provincial fishing provinces.

COMBINED TRANSPORTATION AND TRAVELWAYS PROVINCES

The Right of the Road, Frederick Remington, 1900

Creative province travelways can combine any number of means of travel. Indeed, as province roads start to expand their networks, it will be expedient in many cases to overlap compatible travelways.

Below are some examples of the kinds of combined travelways that might be created or re-created by provincializing.

Example: Old West Province Road

In this example, people create a road for historic travel throughout a Province of the Old American Wild West. The Old West Province Road features all manner of pre-Industrial-Era travel, including stagecoaches, wagon trains, and other horse travel, as well as bicyclists and other pedestrians.

As the Old West Province Road expands, it overlaps in certain places with non-period horse and bicycle province roads.

The Old West Province Road gradually becomes flanked by accommodations catering to its specialized clientele: stables, farriers, wainwrights, and bicycle dealers and repair shops, as well as period inns and cafés.

| *Example: The Heritage Silk Road*

The Silk Road was a network of passageways linking cities and outlying areas throughout Asia, the Indian subcontinent, the Mediterranean Sea, and through Europe and connecting North to the Viking's East Way, at various times in history. It got its name from the lucrative Chinese silk trade, which was carried out along its route beginning during the Han Dynasty (206 BC – 220 AD), primarily by the double-humped Bactrian camel. Its rest stops were called caravan serais. Portions of the ancient road have been designated a UNESCO World Heritage Site. Today, China is implementing an ambitious plan to build a modern Silk Road over land and sea.[4]

In our example, people create a Heritage Silk Road with the Vision of using historic methods of transport—travel by horse, camel, elephant, and other period methods along its land routes, and by historic ship on its sea routes—to trade provincially produced goods. Its rules encourage period dress and customs, and it teams up with various Historic and Heritage Provinces, as well as Industry Provinces, which use it for shipping their fine, handcrafted goods.

Eventually the Heritage Silk Road becomes famed once again for its breathtaking beauty, excitement, and the exquisite goods it brings to the rest of the world.

| *Example: King Edward Travelway*

In this example, people create a province travelway that specializes in the transition period of the early Industrial Era. The King Edward Travelway features fine horse carriages, such as post chaises, barouches, Hansom Cabs, stagecoaches, and early automobiles, as well as historic train lines and early-period airports and planes.

The King Edward Travelway thus becomes a significant network of provincial travelways between various late Nineteenth Century and early Twentieth Century Province outposts. It draws to it, businesses that serve its traveling clientele, such as terminals where people can leave their

---

4. Whether China might include historical means of travel in certain restored sections of the road is unknown at the time of this writing.

modern vehicles behind, and sit in period cafés with vintage menus and the latest provincial news, while waiting for their carriage, train, or biplane.

II. Industry Provinces

The Herring Net, Winslow Homer, 1885

While most Creative Provinces will have one or more industries that their provincials engage in, which relate to their Province Vision, some Provinces will be created with the Primary Vision of creating, promoting, restoring, and protecting a particular industry.

Thus, the definition of an Industry Province:

> **Industry Provinces** *are those where people establish a particular industry as their primary vision.*

Industry Provinces give small and cottage industries a structural tool to compete with the global giants that have been gobbling them up like big fish swallowing the smaller ones. Nature has ways to keep the small fish alive so that both big and small can exist. Likewise, Industry Provinces are a tool to help keep our society vibrant with both large and small enterprises.

Most Creative Provinces will have industries of some type associated with them. Some will have as their Primary Vision, the promotion of a particular type of industry, such as small-scale organic farming. Others will have industries that help support their Primary Vision, such as tourism, hospitality, trade, and real estate. Whether it is a Primary or Supporting Vision, an industry will give strength and longevity to any Creative Province.

Farm and Cottage Industry Provinces

> *A community of small farmers...land property owners, will be the only assurance that the freedom our republic offers will be guaranteed to each and every citizen.*
>
> Thomas Jefferson

Sheep on the Moor, Anton Mauve, 1880

One of the most promising uses for Creative Provinces is to help create, re-establish, protect, and strengthen, small and independent farms and cottage industries.

We have seen many maneuvers by big corporate operations that destroy small farms and cottage industries: in the dairy industry, with the apple growers, in the beer and ale industry, and in the vegetable oil industry, just to name a few.[5]

But in a world of corporate maneuvering, creative provinces give small, human-scaled farms and cottage industries ways to compete and thrive. They also help us restore the rural farm cultures that have been equally destroyed by large-scale industrial farming.

---

5. The writings of Indian economist Vandana Shiva are a good source of information on how some of these maneuvers have been done.

Example: Sunnybrook Home Farm Province

We will define Home Farm Provinces as those in which the traditional small "family farm" is revived, based around homesteads with a garden, and diverse animals and crops. Each farm is small enough to be sustainably managed by the people living on its homestead. Provincials raise a variety of crops and farm animals using traditional methods, which, although they were not originally called such, are diverse, sustainable, and organic.

In this example, a Sunnybrook Home Farm Province is established by a group of diverse small farmers. The Province Vision is to raise farm animals that are pastured, and to bring back the old and sustainable small-farm traditions.

Thus one sees cows in the pasture, chickens running about hunting and pecking for insects and worms; small bands of pigs roaming through orchards that grace the hillsides; geese and ducks swimming in small ponds; barn cats hunting mice; and on some of the farms, work horses pulling wagons and plows.

One of the key Supporting Visions of the Sunnybrook Home Farm Province is to establish cooperative marketing of their farm products, particularly to regional stores.

The Province also revives a traditional family-farm culture, to include old-time country fairs, one-room schoolhouses, group-harvesting activities, picnics, horse-drawn hayrides, and barn-raisings.

Example: The Land of Milk and Honey

Some farm and cottage industry provinces will specialize more than what is described in the Home Farm Province. These farms might be diverse to some degree, to enable them to be self-sufficient; or the farmers may have cooperative arrangements with other farms for various products and supplies.

In this example, independent organic dairy farmers, horticulturists, and beekeepers create The Land of Milk and Honey. The Province is in a hilly region of wild meadows suited to pasturing small dairy herds of cows or goats, and where many of the dairy farms have been around for a century or more.

Likewise, there are small and cottage horticulture operations, especially flower and herb gardening, and beekeeping.

By provincializing, these dairy farmers, horticulturists, and beekeepers connect in a wide swath, creating a region that attracts similar small agricultural operations. Specialty dairies and artisan cheese makers are also drawn to the Province.

The herds are small enough that each cow or goat has a name—Daisy being a favorite—and throughout the province, wildflowers and heaths grow in abundance in and around the pasture land, for the bees and other supporting creatures. Chemical pesticides and microwave-radiating cell towers and the like are prohibited in order to keep the bee colonies (and everyone else) safe. Organic flower gardens and orchards also proliferate, all of which in turn draw yet more specialized cottage industries and provincial arts.

EXAMPLE: COAT OF MANY COLORS ORGANIC COTTON PROVINCE

In this example, a Coat of Many Colors Organic Cotton Province is created by a group of small, organic cotton growers. A viable organic cotton industry develops, and the Province's lands that have been previously depleted by chemical agriculture are revived.

More specialized industries then develop in this Province, including cotton textiles in all manner of designs and colors; provincial clothing designers; and designers of whimsical curtains and upholstery fabrics.

An interesting provincial art develops: Flag makers are drawn to the Province's textile industry, and a sister Winds of Color Flag Province develops. Soon colorful flags line provincial streets and replace signs on buildings. (See the Winds of Color Flag Province example under Artistic and Architectural Concept Provinces for more on this.)

EXAMPLE: CHANTICLEER COTTAGE PROVINCE

Few things are closer to heaven than the free-range backyard hen, herding her baby chicks through the grasses and weeds as she teaches them to scratch for insects, seeds, and worms. And of course, Chanticleer himself, too, crowing in the morning, and protecting his ladies from hawks and other threats.

In this example, a Chanticleer Cottage Province is formed with the Vision of cottages with hens and roosters freely grazing in and between the backyards and gardens. Its cottage industry becomes a main source of eggs to the greater community.

The Province also encourages wild meadows to provide a healthful variety of wild plants, seeds, and bugs for the chickens, as well as a peaceful degree of natural quietude. And adding to the quaintness, the Province's roosters are used instead of alarm clocks to wake people in the morning.

EXAMPLE: AUNT BEA'S KITCHEN GARDEN PROVINCE

In this example, named after Aunt Bea of "Mayberry"[6] fame, a Province is created with the Vision of bringing back the time-honored kitchen garden.

Aunt Bea's Kitchen Garden Province encourages and assists with kitchen gardens in a variety of ways: Provincials share certain garden equipment, and help each other establish gardens with tilling and fence building. It establishes a community kitchen for canning. And it holds an annual Aunt Bea's Fair, with contests to choose the best pies, pickles, and other delectables.

The Province soon boasts many award-wining kitchens and cottage industries. A provincial culture develops that is decidedly Mayberry in its fashions, traditions, and slow-lane life, and eventually it combines with similar provinces to form a larger, Province Federation of Mayberry.

EXAMPLE: DANDELION COTTAGE HERB PROVINCE

Cottage farms are similar to home farms, or family farms, but are smaller in scale, often including just a house and a producing yard.

In this example, we have a Dandelion Cottage Herb Province, specializing in herb culture, with its signature herb

---

6. Mayberry is the fictional North Carolina town featured in "The Andy Griffith Show," with Aunt Bea as one of the main characters.

being the beneficent Dandelion—considered by herbalists to be one of the great "all-heal" herbs.

The Province includes numerous cottage operations where varieties of herbs are gathered in the wild, or organically cultivated, and products, such as herbal tinctures and dried herbs and teas are prepared and sold.

A provincial culture develops that includes provincials collecting flowers from vast fields of bright yellow in the springtime, other herb collecting forages, tincture-making gatherings, and dandelion wine festivals.

The Province eventually draws to it herb teashops and tearooms, herbalists, publishers of books on herb culture and herbal medicine, and supportive operations such as apiaries.

EXAMPLE: THE THREE LITTLE PIGS PROVINCE

In this example, people form a Three Little Pigs Province, a province of homesteads with sizeable yards or small pastures, each of which houses either three pigs; or, those with five pigs, have "This Little Piggy" small pastures.

In the Three Little Pigs cottage farms you'll find pig homes made of straw, sticks, and bricks.

The Province vision is to produce and help market the all-natural pastured pork products of their provincial micro-producers. Traditional meat curing processes are used—in other words, no carcinogenics are allowed.

In addition to meat products, provincials also make pastured pork leaf lard—the wonderful fat for making the best piecrusts; and some provincials have a small industry making the piecrusts for the market.

The Three Little Pigs Province cottage industries grow to a sizeable number of producers, and their Three Little Pigs and This Little Piggy labels are highly prized for their clean and natural products from healthy and happy pastured pigs.

EXAMPLE: BILLY GOATS GRUFF PROVINCE

As well as being a wonderful source of dairy products, goats are excellent for all types of brush control.

In this example, people create a Billy Goats Gruff Province in a hilly countryside area where male goats provide brush control and female goats provide milk for a provincial goat dairy industry.

In this Province, at the end of the season, provincials turn out their teams of goats in the fields and meadows for anyone who wants a sustainable alternative to brush-hogging. In this way, the goats are fed, and the small creatures inhabiting the meadow are preserved.

The Province also has a cottage industry of goat yoga, as well as the added benefit of occasionally getting to see people butted on the behind.

OPEN RANGE, AND WILD FISH, GAME, AND GATHERING PROVINCES

Wild Meat for Wild Men, Charles M. Russell, 1890

Open Range, and Wild Fish, Game, and Gathering Provinces can be created for all manner of herding, fishing, hunting, and gathering operations, such as sheep herding, cattle grazing, wild game hunting, falconry, and berry gathering.

Any number of province rules can be adopted to facilitate the sharing of these open-range province areas. For example, certain limitations might be placed on fencing in provinces of open-range sheep and cattle herding, requiring in their stead, sheep dogs and shepherds, or cowboys. Motorized traffic might be limited or replaced altogether by horses.

> EXAMPLE: RAWHIDE OPEN RANGE PROVINCE
>
> *But early in the twentieth century the herd law that said ranchers must fence in their animals closed the open range, and the confined cattle trampled the grassy verges as they congregated to drink. The banks of the Beaver began to erode and sand washed down into the bed. Within the decade the Beaver was dying and finally stopped flowing except in heavy rains...*
>
> —Annie Proulx, *That Old Ace in the Hole*

The fencing-in of cattle and related confined-herd practices have caused the destruction of many environments, including diverse grasslands and major streams. As any farmer or rancher knows, too many ruminants (or any other species, for that matter) in one area of land will deplete it. But by provincializing, open ranges can be revived and native grasslands and streams can be revitalized.

In this example, a Rawhide Open Range Province is formed with the Vision of reviving traditional open-range cattle herding, cattle drives, and the culture of the cowboy on horseback. One of the Province's Supporting Visions is to develop local abattoirs in key locations to where the Province cattle can be herded on their cattle drives.

The Province membership also includes ecologists who assist with bringing back the native grasses, living streams, and wildlife, and who advise on the best locations for cattle pathways, the timing for cattle drives, and the size of herds.

A viable provincial meat industry develops, together with a revitalization of the traditional cowboy culture.

Example: North Atlantic Independent Fishermen's Province

As with farming, small-scale independent fishermen can create provinces to re-establish and protect their human-scaled industries.

In this example, fishermen in several coastal communities on both sides of the pond form a North Atlantic Independent Fishermen's Province to enable them to join together to compete with large corporate fishing operations. Their Province Vision is to protect their traditional fishing grounds from the latter's giant fishing trawlers.

As the Province grows, provincial industries develop, including traditional net-making using hemp and other biodegradable materials, small-boat building, and traditional fishing tours.

One of the supporting visions of the North Atlantic Independent Fishermen's Province is to reactivate or rebuild historic lighthouses and traditional navigation equipment and, to help accomplish this, they form a federation partnership with the Heritage Lighthouse and Sea Lanes Province described under Water Transportation and Travelways Provinces.

A Province culture develops that revives traditional seafaring cuisine, arts, and festivals, and also creates new activities such as coastal waters cleanup days and marine mammal friendship tours.

| EXAMPLE: NORTH WOODS WILD GAME PROVINCE

In this example, a North Woods Wild Game Province is formed to create a vast region where hunting wild game is a provincial industry that includes meat retail sales, and game-featured restaurants and lodges. The Province assiduously protects its game animals and the viability of their environment, and provincials offer hunter training and safety monitoring to fellow members and visitors.

The Province also teams up with a Wilderness Province Travelway, which features such transportation as small planes and trams to drop off and pick up the hunters.

As the Province grows it also develops sister relationships with various wilderness protection provinces.

| EXAMPLE: HIGHLAND SHEEP AND WOOL PROVINCE

Each lot was led by an old bell wether, who wore the bell fastened to his neck… each bell had a different note, and all had a lovely tone, and could be heard for an immense distance… the sheep knew the note of their own particular wether's bell and would follow it… [B]esides the notes of the…bells was the pleasant calling of the anxious old ewes to their lambs, who… ran and played about amongst themselves, till they thought they were lost, when they called plaintively and raced after their mothers. Each flock was strung out till it was nearly half a mile long as the sheep slowly wended their several miles to their respective heaths.

—Ernest Lewis, *Beth—A Sheep Dog*

In this example, a Highland Sheep and Wool Province is formed with the Vision of creating a vast area for raising sheep that are open-grazed, and to encourage provincial wool and meat industries.

The provincial industries that develop include markets and restaurants that feature lamb; wool spinning and weaving; and the training of border collies and other sheep dogs, which are used extensively in the Province.

Provincial cultural activities include collie sheep-herding competitions; sheep-shearing competitions; exhibitions of pastoral art and wool artisanship; and restaurants featuring lamb cuisine.

Example: The Village Shepherd Province

On a smaller scale from the Highland Sheep Herding and Wool Province is the example of the Village Shepherd Province.

This Province is created in a semi-rural village setting where vast mowed lawns exist. The Province Vision is to replace much of the lawns with pasture: the grasses around houses are grazed by sheep, the way it used to be done.

The Province Master Shepherd is an elected position, but there are other shepherds as well, and border collies to herd the sheep. Motorized traffic is diverted where the sheep are grazing.

Provincials each own sheep, but communal grazing is done on all the provincial lands, and provincials devise a plan for sharing the bounty of wool and meat. Spring lambing, and sheep shearing become Province cultural events.

Example: Black Bear Gathering Province

In Gathering Provinces, provincials share in the gathering of Nature's wild bounty. Such provinces might combine in their memberships, tracts of land that have wild areas with desired plants, or perhaps lands that need to be revived of their food-bearing plants.

In this example, people create a Black Bear Gathering Province for gathering native wild fruits, herbs, and mushrooms. The Province Vision is also to "give back" to Nature and her wildlife. Thus, in addition to its gathering activities, provincials monitor the food supply of their wildlife, particularly the Province's signature animal, the Black Bear, and help propagate native berry bushes, fruit trees, and other indigenous edible plants.

WORKING ANIMAL PROVINCES:
GIVING ANIMALS BACK THEIR JOBS

Elephant biem Arbeiten, Digitalpress

Every job on Earth has a creature made to do that very thing! Why should we use poisons to keep aphids off our plants when we can use Ladybugs? Why should we use traps and poisons to control rodent populations when cats and dogs would love to do the job for us, and catch their own dinner besides? And why should we spray poison in our communities for mosquitoes, or set up artificial traps, when frogs, fish, bats, and countless other creatures are starving for a few billion of them?

Working Animal Provinces are provinces where animals are featured to do any of these particular jobs, and countless more.

EXAMPLE: LAOS WORKING ELEPHANT PROVINCE

Throughout the Indian subcontinent and much of Asia, the intelligent, gentle Asian Elephant has been the traditional partner of man for heavy work and travel.

In this example, a Laos (Land of a Million Elephants) Working Elephant Province is created with the Vision of maintaining elephants in their traditional working roles. The Province encourages the training of elephants and their handlers, and facilitates their hiring for various jobs, such as heavy work in construction and demolition, and for heritage pageants.

One of the Supporting Visions of the Province is to provide places where working elephants can be returned for respite and for retirement, reuniting them with their families. Another Supporting Vision of this province is to maintain habitats that can sustainably support elephants, and the Province has in its membership ecologists who assist with this.

EXAMPLE: WORKING DOG PROVINCE

There are probably as many jobs that dogs do, as there are breeds of dogs. Hunting, guarding, tracking, guiding, retrieving, herding...these are just some of the main categories of jobs.

In this example, dog-lovers create a Working Dog Province with the Vision of a community where trained dogs and their trainers live and share various resources.

To join the Province, provincials demonstrate a degree of dog training ability, and have dogs that are well trained to not only follow commands, but to do a specific job. Among the provincials are current and former K-9 police officers, combat soldiers with war dogs, detectives with working bloodhounds, shepherds with border collies, and many more.

The provincial dogs are so well behaved they hardly need any fencing or leashing. Dog parks abound, as well as dog cafés, grooming spas, and many services such as placement agencies.

Specialty services, such as tracking lost people or animals, become viable industries in the Working Dog Province. There was a time when dogs were used universally to track down missing people—before the advent of electronic tracking devices. But any advantages of electronic chips and the like are far outweighed by their disadvantages: a dystopian world where some entity imbeds an electronic chip in your body, by which this unknown entity is able to control your life.

In contrast, the great benefits of tracking dogs are that they are *not* controlling, invasive, pervasive, unknown, unaccountable, and unalive. They are loving, living creatures—partners of humans, who do their job very well, and love to do it!

Example: Cat and Mouse Province

Cats perform the important job of patrolling the farm or neighborhood to keep the rodent population in check. And rodents perform the important job of feeding cats! (And many other species, too.)

In this example, people create a Cat and Mouse Province where cats, together with their normal rodent prey—mice, moles and voles, are encouraged in a balanced, synergistic environment. These provincials don't have to buy cat food! Or not much, anyway. Another step toward Freedom.

Also, old-time rat-catchers make a good living here providing food for elderly cats and dogs who might not be able to hunt on their own.

Example: Bat City

Individuals of some bat species can capture up to 1,000 mosquitoes in a single hour, and large colonies can consume amazing quantities. For example, a Florida colony of 30,000 southeastern bats was calculated to capture 50 tons of insects annually, including over 15 tons of mosquitoes.[7]

Bats are one of the great insectivores, and in this example, they are put to work in a Bat City Province, created in a metropolitan area that abuts a river. The bats are encouraged and protected, and are used as the primary method of mosquito control.

Likewise, mosquitoes are kept in a synergistic balance with the bats, and misguided attempts to kill off this critical food source are dispensed with. People use screens on their porches and windows, and citronella products become a viable industry here.

The Province takes advantage of the classic Batman comic book and television series characters to create its culture. Its domain is called Gotham, and Batman, Robin, and Batgirl are honorary provincial positions. The Province has a synergistic relationship with the local police, and Batmobiles patrol the streets.

---

7. From Bat Conservation and Management, www.batmanagement.com, September 9, 2020.

Manufacturing Provinces

In the Carpenter Shop, Carl Larsson, 1905

Manufacturing Provinces are those created by people with similar manufacturing visions and Complementary skills. Some creative provinces will have a manufacturing Primary Vision. For example, a Province of the North Pole might form with the Primary Vision of toymaking. Other Provinces will often have manufacturing Supporting Visions, such as a Medieval Province that features period cobblers, costumers, swordsmiths, and candlewrights.

> *Example: Oak Hills Artisan Furniture Province*
> In this example, independent furniture craftsmen begin an Oak Hills Artisan Furniture Province, in a region where this craft has been traditionally practiced. The Province Vision is to cooperatively market independently made furniture, and to provide other kinds of provincial support to their furniture craftsmen. Thus the Province creates a marketing brand and business, "Oak Hills Artisan Furniture," under which its independent craftsmen have their own signature products.

Related artists, artisans and businesses, such as upholsterers, furniture sellers, furniture repairers, interior designers, painters, and marketers, also join the Province. It develops a culture that includes provincial festivals and trade shows, as well as schools for learning the furniture-making and design crafts.

Example: The North Pole

In this example of how enchanting a creative province can be, toy-makers and Yule/Christmas/Hanukah artisans join together to form a Province of The North Pole in a quaint northern setting.

Santa and Mrs. Claus run the toy-making and toy-distribution operation, and provincials of small stature are the Elves who have key roles in both management and designing and making the toys.

Travel within the Province is by snowshoe, pony, sleigh, skis, and of course reindeer. Eventually a Polar Express Train[8] is built to carry provincial visitors to The North Pole.

While Santa's headquarters are in this North Pole Province, numerous corollary Santa Claus Provinces and Christmas Provinces also form around the globe, with their many outpost Santas, glittering Christmas shops, candlelit Hanukah shops, Christmas tree farms, and toy-making operations. Together these provinces form a Santa Claus Province Federation. The Santas of the federation select the head Santa Claus, like cardinals selecting the pope.

Example: Post-Detroit Motor Vehicle Manufacturing Province

In this example, independent vehicle designers and builders, seeing the beginnings of a viable provincial vehicle industry, form a Post-Detroit Motor Vehicle Manufacturing Province. The Province Vision is for independent designers and builders of motor vehicles of all types to join together to collectively design, build, restore, and market vehicles for the various emerging provincial markets.

---

8. Based on the book *The Polar Express*, by Chris Van Allsburg, Houghton Mifflin, 1985.

The provincial markets include: early-Twentieth Century automobile reproductions for historic and heritage provinces; uniquely designed vehicles for certain concept provinces, such as yellow solar powered vehicles for a Sunshine Province; and tiny electric vehicles for All-Electric Provinces.

The Province begins in and around Detroit, the old center of the American automobile industry, but eventually expands to many provincial hubs around the world that have specialized vehicle markets.

Post-Detroit also develops a provincial culture of its own, which includes, among other things, trade shows, festivals, and a revival of Mo-Town music.

Eventually, Post-Detroit, and other provincial vehicle manufacturing provinces, form a Federation of Provincial Vehicle Manufacturing Provinces.

EXAMPLE: YE OLDE SHIPBUILDING PROVINCE

In this example, independent shipbuilders and designers create Ye Olde Shipbuilding Province. The Province Vision is for independent shipbuilders, restorers, and designers to join together to collectively build, restore, and market pre-industrial-era ships and boats of all kinds for the emerging historic and heritage provincial markets.

Ye Olde Shipbuilding Province makes and restores historic watercraft of all types, including tall ships, riverboats, ironclads, and ocean liners.

Ye Olde Shipbuilding Province also belongs to, and becomes an integral sector of, many historic and heritage provinces around the globe.

EDUCATION AND RESEARCH PROVINCES

On a Visit to the Teacher, Nikolay Bogdanov Belsky

Education and Research Provinces are those created by people with similar teaching, learning, and investigative visions and Complementary skills. Some creative provinces will have education or research as their primary vision, focusing on a certain subject or field, such as music education or astronomical research. Others might be created as an alternative to state-controlled schools.

Still others might form around a particular investigative project, such as an archeological site. In that case, a provincial industry might form around a college or archeological dig, in order to expand that endeavor's sphere by adding residences, businesses, corollary research projects, and the like.

Investigation Provinces might also be formed to monitor and continue an investigation initially done by a government body, when people are not satisfied with the government's results. Such creative provinces might also serve as citizen's ombudsmen or protected areas for whistleblowers.

Many creative provinces might have supporting visions that include education and research endeavors. Indeed, probably most will include instruction of various kinds for both provincials and visitors.

> EXAMPLE: DOWN-THE-LANE SCHOOLHOUSE PROVINCE

State-controlled education is one of the best examples of using government for far too many tasks. People can rectify this situation by creating provinces to educate their children as they see fit.

In this example, a group of home-school parents form a Down-the-Lane Schoolhouse Province, with the vision of directing the course of their children's education, in a small, neighborhood school. The one-room schoolhouse is located nearby where the children can walk to school, and either walk home for lunch, or take their lunch with them. The teachers are skilled in all levels of primary and secondary education, and older children help the younger ones with many tasks.

There is no connection to any government-mandated curriculum at Down the Lane; rather, the parents meet regularly to work on the students' curriculum. The result is a specialized education suited to the vision of the parents.

> EXAMPLE: SITCHIN ANTEDILUVIAN RESEARCH PROVINCE

In this example, archeologists and other scholars of Humanity's most ancient texts and cultures form a Sitchin Antediluvian Research Province, named after the late scholar, Zechariah Sitchin. The Vision of the Province is to study and preserve the texts, history, artifacts, and archeological sites of Humanity's origins, forming a provincial university.

The Province grows to include a number of public and private museums, and antediluvian archeological sites such as Sumer, Babylon, and the Ark on Mt. Ararat.

> EXAMPLE: MICROWAVE RADIATION INVESTIGATION PROVINCE

In this example, people in a community where illnesses have skyrocketed after the installation of cell towers, form a Microwave Radiation Investigation Province after government investigators conclude that the cell towers do not affect their residents' health.

The provincials collect their own evidence to present in court, and ultimately succeed in getting the cell towers and similar dangerous technologies removed from their Province areas.

Health Provinces

> *The power of community to create health is far greater than any physician, clinic, or hospital.*
> Dr. Mark Hyman

Freepik.com

Health Provinces are those that have a particular health industry or health outlook as their Primary Vision.

Such creative provinces might focus on such things as learning healthy lifestyles, a particular healing protocol, or a care-giving service. Or they may be restful enclaves for healing and convalescence, or places where people with similar illnesses get mutual support, healthful dietary and exercise regimens, and easy access to health specialists.

While there are many health centers today that specialize in these things, they are often not accessible to many would-be patrons because they are either too expensive, too far away, or are not covered under the patron's insurance plan.

Health specialists would be drawn to such provinces, and would be able to learn from each other and the provincial patients.

Example: Natural Health Province

In this example, healers and other people who offer, teach, support, or follow naturopathic health protocols form a Natural Health Province. Their Primary Vision is to promote natural methods for health, such as nutrition, chiropractic, herbal medicine, midwifery, homeopathy, natural surgery, acupuncture, electronic medicine, fasting, and cleansing. Since the early twentieth century there has been a suppression, and even the outlawing, of many of these health protocols, brought on by big money interests influencing governments to overstep their bounds.

The Natural Health Province, as it grows, brings into its membership, many naturopathic schools and practitioners, and it becomes a pillar in the health community for advancing the strengthening of the immune system. The Province includes some small, health-oriented hospitals that provide restful environments for healing, including healthful food, and natural-light and dark-night, quiet rooms.

Example: Living Earth Raw Foods Province

Nature's diet of organic, raw foods has been rediscovered as a diet for health and longevity. But because many cultures have lost the techniques for preparing delicious raw dishes, creative provinces that specialize in this cuisine could be very helpful.

In this example, a Living Earth Raw-Foods Province is formed with the Vision of specializing in raw foods cuisine. The Province has among its members, restaurateurs, chefs, teachers, and nutritionists, as well as provincials who just want to learn and follow the diet.

Soon the Living Earth Province contains many restaurants, cuisine schools, and health practitioners. Numerous organic farms join their ranks, and many provincials also have cottage gardens, all of which provide food for the restaurants, as well as places where Province visitors can stay.

Eventually the Living Earth Raw-Foods Province connects with the Garden of Eden Province (see its description under Historic and Heritage Provinces).

EXAMPLE: RESTORE HEALTH CLEANSING PROVINCE

Cleansing has been very neglected in modern cultures, contributing greatly to all manner of bodily corruption and disease. But awareness of its critical role is reemerging.

In this example, cleansing professionals form a Restore Health Cleansing Province, with the Vision of teaching and practicing the many methods of eradicating all kinds of bodily corruption.

Thus, in the Restore Health Cleansing Province, provincials provide guidance and hands-on assistance to people for such cleansing protocols as full-body parasite cleansing, liver flushing, herbal dissolving of kidney stones, sinus cleansing, heavy metal removal, chelation, toxic chemical avoidance, radiation avoidance, and the many kinds of fasting.

Thus, in the provincial setting, these powerful healing techniques become more available to the average person.

III. Environment Provinces

Morning in a Pine Forest, Konstantin Savitsky and Ivan Shishkin

All Creative Provinces will have a physical environment in which to live, work, and/or travel, and will define these environments in their Supporting Visions. But some provinces will be created with the Primary Vision of creating, promoting, restoring, or protecting a particular environment.

Thus, the definition of an Environment Province:

> ***Environment Provinces*** *are those where people establish a particular environment as their primary vision.*

Thus, Environment Provinces can be formed to create a certain kind of environment, such as a type of landscape; to promote certain environmental practices, such as organic gardening or a type of energy; to restore and protect a particular environment, such as a wilderness or a body of water; to protect a particular species, such as Monarch butterflies; or to establish a certain state of being, such as natural quietude or clean air.

Garden Provinces

Garden Provinces are those that have a Vision to create a garden environment of some kind. Garden Provinces can be provinces of private gardens, communal gardens, public gardens, or any combination thereof.

Garden Provinces differ from Farm and Cottage Industry Provinces in that their Primary Vision is to create a particular garden environment, rather than to create gardens specifically as industries. You will also see that there is a great deal of overlapping between garden provinces and architectural concept provinces, and it will be up to the provincial creators what their emphasis is to be.

Like the automobile dominating the world's transportation, the "mowed lawn" has taken over much of the western world's residential, public, and commercial parkland spaces, with the result that we have inadvertently created a very extensive "Lawn Province." There is nothing wrong with lawns—indeed, they create parklands and also beautify a garden, and make it accessible. But the *excess* of lawns can result in their displacing much

Roses Arch in the Garden, by Joshua Haviv

of our natural meadows and other types of landscapes, along with their countless beneficial species. But now we can think outside the "lawn box" and create beautiful and magical Garden Provinces.

Garden Provinces will no doubt be among the most beautiful of the creative provinces. They might specialize in certain types of flowers, such as roses, lilies, tulips, or phlox. They may focus on a certain garden design feature such as stonewalls, archways, rock gardens, water gardens, or living fences.

There might be creative provinces of abodes of living roofs, or a Topiary Province might be created by gardeners interested in creating a community setting of living sculpture.

Other garden provinces may pattern themselves after famous gardens, such as Claude Monet's home, Giverny.

Like other creative provinces, Garden Provinces will develop provincial cultures, such as the revival of the ancient Language of Flowers: using specific flowers to convey messages.

Example: Old Rose Heritage Garden Province

In this example, an Old Rose Heritage Garden Province is created with the Vision of encouraging the cultivation of old rose varieties. These old roses, such as the Eden Rose, are very hardy and require no synthetic pesticides to survive.

Throughout the Province there are pathways with arches, fences, and arbors covered with cascading climbing roses of gorgeous scent. Ladybugs are used for aphid control, and everywhere there are bees gathering nectar.

A Rose Committee of Master Rose Gardeners runs the Province. Provincials develop a micro-industry of rose oil, potpourri, and other rose products.

Example: Old Possum Orchard Province

In this example, an Old Possum Orchard Province is begun in an area where people want to reestablish backyard fruit trees and wildlife.

Fruit trees are planted in residential gardens, and on some properties larger orchards are planted. Throughout the Province there are occasional clearings in the orchards where there are beautifully designed picnic tables where provincials meet for tea and pie.

A provincial culture develops around the planting and harvesting of fruit, orchard picnics, and of course the fruit-loving Possum.

Example: Sleepy Hollow Woodland Province

In this example, a Sleepy Hollow Woodland Province is started in an existing neighborhood that was originally built in a woodland setting, but which over time had been subjected to the trends of asphalt and lawns. The Province Vision is to restore the original woodland setting, and to protect its natural resources, including its streams, wildlife, dark skies, and natural quietude.

Woods and gardens of coralbells, hostas, vinca, lungwort, violets, astilbe, bleeding hearts, impatiens, and other shade-dwelling flora surround the houses, and there are earthen footpaths leading the walker through paths of lilies of the valley, from one dwelling to another, and to magical glens of rustic wood benches and tables.

At night, glens are alighted with faerie lights, and owls, frogs, nightingales, and other night creatures call out softly from their sylvan abodes.

Example: Pooh and Friends Backyard Wildlife Province

In a proto-province example, the National Wildlife Federation has created the NWF Certified Wildlife Habitat Program to encourage people to create backyard and other habitats helpful to wildlife.

In our example, people create a Pooh and Friends Backyard Wildlife Province, named after A. A. Milne's beloved children's book character. The Province Vision is to create wildlife environments in private backyards and other outdoor areas, using Pooh and similar children's book wildlife characters for its inspiration, and to teach children to be good stewards of wildlife.

Provincial homeowners and businesses establish all kinds of wildlife-friendly grounds, with creative bird houses and feeders, small living ponds and bathing fountains, and plenty of fruit trees, berry-producing shrubs, wild grasses, and other plants wild animals love.

A provincial industry develops of artisans making enchanting wildlife houses and feeders—everything from Winnie the Pooh bear huts, to *Wind in the Willows*-inspired Toad Hall. The Province also includes some farms and cottage industries that specialize in wild bird seed and fruit trees and shrubs, and pots of honey.

The Pooh and Friends Province also develops a sister relationship with an Uncle Remus Province, and together they form a Backyard Children's Fairy Tale Province Federation.

Example: Queen of the Prairie Province

In this example, a Queen of the Prairie Province is started in an area where there used to be a vast prairie of indigenous grasses and meadows teaming with wildlife, including buffalo and horses. The Vision of the Province is to restore the prairie's grasslands and meadows for sustainable grazing, hunting, gathering, and living.

The Province takes its name from the stately and gorgeous flower that rises above the other prairie flora in midsummer to bloom like feathery vibrant-pink flags. This and other wildflowers abound in the Province, as do endless sources of other wild plants and animals for food and other uses, all of which help keep the prairie alive and thriving.

A Province culture develops around sustainable hunting and gathering activities of the prairie's many wild offerings. Many provincials also partake in prairie heritage arts, such as quilting.

Provincials take pride in retrofitting their homes and surrounding land to fit into the prairie landscape, and one can sometimes see buffalo meandering through backyard meadows, and wild mustangs galloping in the distance. And everywhere, in the height of summer, the Queen of the Prairie blooms and reigns.

Environmental Concept Provinces

Starry Night Over the Rhone, Dang Do Anh Thinh, 1888

Most creative provinces will have environmental concepts among their Supporting Visions: the ways in which the provincials want to fashion the environment in which they live, work, and travel. But some will have an environmental concept as their Primary Vision. Thus a Creative Province might be formed with the primary purpose of creating natural quietude, dark skies, or an organic environment. Or the province might want to create a special environment in which to accomplish something, such as a peaceful memorial setting, or children's creative backyards.

Example: Milky Way Dark Skies Province

In this example, people in a prairie setting decide to take advantage of its big skies to create a Milky Way Dark Skies Province. Some of the Province's founders are also involved with a nearby observatory. Their Vision is to restore and promote natural nighttime darkness for environmental, stargazing, health, and aesthetic purposes, and to promote stargazing and astronomy.

In the Province, outdoor artificial light is strictly limited: Down-lighting is used where street lighting is deemed necessary, and motion-detection lights and dogs are employed for security.

The Province draws to it all manner of stargazing activities, star mapping, star arts, and the many astronomical studies. Provincials become very astute at knowing the sky. Dark-sky industries are drawn to the Province, including telescope manufacturing, star maps, star art, and schools of astronomy and astrology.

Example: Birdsong Province

In this example, a Birdsong Province has as its Primary Vision, a Soundscape of Natural Quietude and Birdsong.

To achieve this, the Province limits mechanical noise that extends beyond one's property line, by decibel level, duration, and time of day.

Secondly, the Province encourages songbirds, with the reestablishment of wild meadows, wildflower plantings, hedges, hedgerows, and other natural sources of songbird food and shelter; and it limits toxic chemicals and electromagnetic frequencies that are harmful to birds. It also encourages bird feeders in a way that enhances but does not replace the birds' natural food sources.

Thirdly, the Province adjusts outdoor lighting to be unobtrusive, so that it does not hinder birds, and also so that provincials can sleep with their windows open.

What develops is a heavenly Province of birdsong in daylight. At night, the soft lullabies of such birds as owls, nightingales, mockingbirds, whip-poor-wills, thrushes, and night herons sing provincials to sleep. And at daybreak, provincials awaken to the magnificent dawn chorus of warblers, robins, thrush, wrens, cardinals, and many other songbird species, singing through their open windows.

Example: Alive Biogenic Province

In this example, an Alive Biogenic Province is created with a Vision of using living beings to accomplish as many tasks, and to fulfill as many functions, as possible.

Thus provincials live in living structures such as tree houses or earthen houses with grass and sedum roofs. They eat a largely raw-foods diet. Ants, skunks, and other cleanup species are used for cleaning many things. Living, dirt roads replace asphalt and concrete. Horses, donkeys, and other transport creatures are used for transportation. Workhorses and oxen are employed in farming. Messages are delivered by messenger—human or other creature. Dogs guard the premises and perform many other tasks. Cats keep the rodent population in synergistic balance. Fences and sculpture are made of living things such as shrubbery. Entertainment is live. News is spread via town crier and wandering minstrel.

EXAMPLE: FRESH AIR CLOTHESLINE PROVINCE

There are a number of household chemicals that contribute to local air pollution, but, because everyone does laundry, the most pervasive are probably laundry chemicals emitted via clothes dryers.

So, in this example, people form a Fresh Air Clothesline Province. Here the air is sweet, fresh, and clean enough that you want to hang your laundry outdoors to dry. Provincials use laundry products that are toxin-free, and create certain rules on the use of clothes dryers.

The Province is very colorful and quaint. Clothesline art is well honed, and there are competitions for the most beautiful clothesline displays. A cottage industry also develops of decorative clothespins and clothesline separators, wool dryer balls, and clotheslines.

EXAMPLE: EASTER PASSION SACRED GROVE

One beautiful way to honor the dead is with a Sacred Grove Province. Differing from classic cemeteries, Sacred Groves are gardens, orchards, vineyards, or wildernesses where the dead are either buried or are honored with monuments or other memorials of some type. By turning these spaces into memorial grounds for people or animals, they are made sacred. Such creative provinces can thus be a way to help preserve old growth forests and other environmental treasures.

Sacred Groves might feature a certain type of plant, such as Christmas trees or grape vines; or they might feature a certain type of garden architecture, such as arbors or stone archways; or they might honor a certain kind of person, such as in an Orphan's Sacred Grove; or they might honor a type of animal, as in a Companion Animal Sacred Grove or an Elephant Graveyard.

An example of a current intentional community with such a sacred grove is the Windward Community in Oregon, which stewards the Herland Forest Natural Burial Cemetery.

Herland Forest is dedicated to stewarding the reintegration of humans with the Earth in a simple and holistic manner and providing individuals or families opportunity to create meaningful ceremony to honor the lives of their beloveds. Home to towering Ponderosa pines and ancient Oregon white oaks, migratory birds, fungi, coyote, and everything in between, Herland is also protecting the forest from future development.[1]

In our example of an Easter Passion Sacred Grove, it is created with the Vision of a quiet, organic, and motor-free province, featuring fruit-tree orchards and other fruit- or nut-producing, spring-blooming plants. The Province has many fruited vines where, instead of headstones, archways and arbors are inscribed with the names of the beloved. Fruit trees, nut trees, spring blooming shrubs, or banks of flowers are planted in honor of the dead, with inscriptions written on small plaques.

To visit a loved ones' burial place, monument, or marker, Province visitors walk, ride a bicycle, or take a horse-drawn carriage. Throughout the Province there are benches and meditative gardens. Some of the fruits and nuts from the trees are left for wildlife, and some are sold by provincials.

The Province culture includes gardening activities, burials, horse-drawn carriage tours to visit gravesites, and Easter and springtime celebrations to honor the dead.

---

1. "Taking Death by the Hand," by Lindsay Hagamen, *Communities— Life in Cooperative Culture*, Issue 172, Fall 2016.

Environmental Restoration and Preservation Provinces

Linda Cook DeVona, book cover of *Bridge Over Willow River*, Illume Publications, courtesy of Jerry Rudnitskiy, author

Creative provinces can be formed to restore and preserve wildernesses, bodies of water, other geological features, and natural states of being, beyond what are currently preserved by governments, private organizations, and individuals.

Provincials can make their own land properties, sea vessels, airplanes, land vehicles, and personal participation a key part of greater efforts to help the environment. Thus, such creative provinces will become natural restoration areas, wilderness buffer zones, links to larger wilderness parks, wildlife corridors, and watch zones.

Environmental Restoration and Preservation Provinces can be invaluable in any place, small or large, that needs environmental help: to revive prairies and meadows; to clean polluted bodies of water; to remove harmful, obsolete dams; to restore wetlands, forests, and jungles; and to restore natural states of being, such as natural quietude.

EXAMPLE: WILLOW CREEK PROVINCE

In this example, people create a Willow Creek Province with the Vision of restoring and protecting the water quality and aquatic life of a local stream, as well as restoring it as a local travelway. Provincials work to remove several obsolete dams that are preventing not only watercraft travel, but also the migration of critical aquatic species such as the eel, and they assiduously monitor and protect the stream.

The Province is run by a committee that includes stream ecologists, wetland biologists, and recreation and stream-travel planners.

A Province culture develops that includes canoe races and other watercraft events, creek-side picnics, and the old fashioned swimming hole complete with rope swings.

EXAMPLE: PINEY WOODS PROVINCE

Davis' plan was to buy up and re-longleaf the "in-between open spaces east of Eglin [Air Force Base] and west of a protected river corridor." He bought 51,000 acres of degraded farm and wood lands, and set about to replant the native species. He has named the land Nokuse Plantation, Nokuse [pronounced "No-GO-see"] being the term for "bear" in the language of the Muskogee, the Native American tribe who once lived there.[2]

M. C. Davis has an ambitious plan to revive the Piney Woods, the "signature ecosystem" of the American South-

---

2. "Can the World Really Set Aside Half the Planet for Wildlife?" Tony Hiss, *Smithsonian Magazine*, September 2014.

east that once spanned sixty percent of its land from Virginia to East Texas.

In our example, a Piney Woods Province is formed by people who want to enhance Davis' plan of recreating a connected primeval forest in the Old South. Provincials include their properties in the scheme, adding many wild-friendly acres to the forest. In this Province there are many residences, but each one is committed to providing friendly habitats to the black bear, the gopher tortoise, and the other critical Piney Woods species.

EXAMPLE: WORMWOOD EXTENSIVE WILDERNESS PROVINCE

In another ambitious example, people create a Wormwood Extensive Wilderness Province with the Vision of connecting wildernesses to extend around their continent. Gradually they create a connected, meandering wilderness of extant and revivified forests and other wild spaces. But unlike wilderness parks that people just visit, in Wormwood, provincials own property and live there, and do all the good works that are needed.

The Province takes its name from the healing herb, also called artemesia, which obsolete is used for cleansing the alimentary tract of parasites. Thus Wormwood includes regions where wildernesses are being revivified—a cathartic process, not unlike the restoring of the body's gut by removing harmful toxins and parasites, and replenishing the beneficial species of the body's microbiome. Of course the provincials are a key part of this Earth microbiome.

The Province culture includes a plethora of wilderness revivification activities, including obdam and hardscape removal, forest and meadow replanting, and the reintroduction of indigenous species.

EXAMPLE: PACIFIC RIM OCEAN RESTORATION PROVINCE

In yet another ambitious example, people around the Pacific Ocean form a Pacific Rim Ocean Restoration Province, with the Vision of its complete environmental restoration.

Provincials include individuals, government agencies, and private organizations who work together to decommission nuclear power plants along the Ocean's shores; end naval sonar sound pollution; end chemical and plastic pollution from seagoing vessels; and revive ocean aquatic species.

The Province is run by a Provincial Board of ocean scientists and activists, and boasts a large Environmental Watch, made up of dedicated provincials who have, among their heritage treasures, many ships, aircraft, and land vehicles.

Example: The Lord's Blessing Farmland Restoration Province

In this example, a group of people looks out upon their heritage lands and sees endless mechanically- and chemically-produced fields of genetically modified corn, owned and run by corporate agriculture. But some of it is now up for sale. The soil has been depleted of living creatures and nutrients, and the streams are polluted. Most of the wildlife is gone, as is the once-vibrant farm community. There are now a few roadside bars and a couple of big-box stores to service a small population of low-paid workers.

This group of people decides to create a Lord's Blessing Farmland Restoration Province, with the Vision of taking back this land, small parcel by small parcel, and reviving it with sustainable, small-farm practices and a supportive, family-farm community.

As The Lord's Blessing Province grows, it recreates many small, sustainable, and diverse home farms. These provincial farms bring the soil back to life, and revive the small ponds and streams. The wildlife returns, families come back to the farms of their ancestors, and the small community schoolhouses and churches are filled once more.

As discussed previously, farm provinces will usually be classified under Industry Provinces—but such categorization will depend on the Primary Vision. In the Lord's Blessing Province, the provincials decide that thanking God for the opportunity to restore the land that had been lost, must always be their Primary Vision.

Featured Animal Provinces

The Tiger, Richard Friese, 1890

Featured Animal Provinces are those where a type of animal is encouraged, protected, and honored. These creative provinces will often be places where a unique habitat exists for a particular species.

Featured Animal Provinces include those that have as their Primary Vision the preservation of certain wild animals; the establishment of animal sanctuaries or rehabilitation enclaves; or the featuring of certain companion animals.

A wonderful proto-creative province of this type is the Atlantic shoreline community of Chincoteague, Virginia, which has successfully protected its wild pony population and included it in its local culture. Chincoteague houses a wildlife refuge for the ponies along its stretch of pristine beach, holds an annual pony swim, and includes the ponies in many of its cultural activities and arts.

As discussed earlier, animals will also feature in many Transportation and Travelways Provinces, and in many Industry Provinces. Such categorization will depend on the creative province's Primary Vision.

Example: Bengal Tiger Province

Another example of a featured-animal proto-province is the Snow Leopard Trust[3] in Mongolia, China, Kyrgyzstan, India, and Pakistan. There the Trust has formed a partnership with the traditional nomadic herding communities, who subsist on their livestock, to protect the now-endangered Snow Leopard instead of hunting it, and to protect the mountain ecosystem. In exchange, the Trust assists the herding communities with earning supplemental income through their traditional wool-working skills.

In our example, people in a region where there are forests containing Bengal tigers form a Bengal Tiger Province, with the Vision of helping to bring back probably the most magnificent creature on Earth to sustainable levels.

The Bengal Tiger Province collects in its membership government protected forests, tiger reserves, wildlife sanctuaries, and very importantly, many private properties that help to both enlarge the tiger's domain and establish large buffer zones and migration corridors for keeping the tigers from more densely populated areas.

The Bengal Tiger Province also becomes a place for zoologists and other professionals to live and study the tiger in the wild, and to rehabilitate captive tigers and reintroduce them into the protected forests. The Province hosts wildlife tours as a provincial industry.

Example: Swan Lakes Province

In this beautiful example, a Swan Lakes Province is formed by people who live around a region of lakes that has a natural habitat suited to swans. The Province Vision is to encourage swans to re-inhabit the lakes region, to restore their population to historic levels, to strengthen or expand swan migration corridors, and to honor the swan and make it the focus of the Province culture.

---

3. www.snowleopard.org

Provincials gradually restore swans to their lakes and make their province a swan sanctuary. Provincials in the arts establish a ballet theater on the shores of one of the lakes, and use Tchaikovsky's Swan Lake ballet as their signature performance.

For more on this concept, see the Swan Lakes example in Part 3, Create Your Primary Vision.

EXAMPLE: WINGS OF FREEDOM PROVINCE

An example of an animal refuge province, is a Wings of Freedom Province: a bird rehabilitation province for bringing caged and injured birds back to a wild or semi-wild state.

The Province collects in its membership, provincials who are specialists in bird rehabilitation, along with aviaries in many locations for birds in transition to the wild state.

The Province becomes a vast network of aviaries, avian rehabilitation specialists, and wild colonies of rehabilitated canaries, parrots, and every other kind of bird imaginable.

EXAMPLE: EDUCATED AND TRAINED FREE-ANIMAL PROVINCE

We've all heard of the famous gorilla, Ko-Ko, and there are many other examples of educated and trained animals with whom humans are able to communicate.

Inspired by Ko-Ko, people create an Educated and Trained Free-Animal Province, with a Vision of training animals so that those not living in the wild are able to completely do away with cages, corrals, leashes, and other confinements, except for training. And how intelligent they discover these animals to be!

The provincials who make up this province become highly skilled at training animals, and the animals also train and educate other animals, of their own and other species. Communication between different species becomes highly developed.

Many of the animals have their own small and rustic homes—huts, bird houses, dog houses, sheds, aquatic homes, and more—which add additional charm to this Province.

Example: Lance Corporal Carrier Pigeon Province

In this example, a Lance Corporal Carrier Pigeon Province is formed with the Vision of creating extensive messenger routes for homing pigeons.

The provincials breed and train the pigeons, and help establish other breeders and handlers, resulting in a wide swath of pigeon messenger routes. The Province develops a culture around the pigeon, with pigeon art, breeding competitions, and messenger races.

An enterprising micro-industry of sending messages also develops.

Example: Marine Mammal Friends Province

In this example, a Marine Mammal Friends Province is formed with the Vision of expanding human communication with wild marine mammals, and both teaching them and learning from them, all without confining them. The provincial students and teachers, both marine mammals and human, attend Province classes, and then are released after their "school day" is through.

Example: Snoopy Province

So much fun can be had with dog provinces! In this example, people in a neighborhood with lots of dogs form a Snoopy Province, with the Vision of creating "a dog-friendly environment of friendly dogs."

In the Snoopy Province, doghouses of various designs are seen in every property. An extensive dog park and a meandering dog run are created, with dog toys, dog playground, and an obstacle course, as well as an adjacent Snoopy Café where owners can sip their coffee or wine while Snoopy runs about playing with his friends. The Province also holds an annual training competition.

Provincial cottage industries develop that include a thriving Doggy Day Care, dog houses of creative designs, and dog training and dog walking services.

Example: Catwalk Province

In this fun example, people in a neighborhood that includes single-family dwellings and condominium complexes create a Catwalk Province, with the Vision of creating a vast network of catwalks and cat doors—high up where cats instinctively like to be. Cats reach these heights via trees, carpeted poles, and cat-sized decorative planks and stairways.

The cats come and go as they please, prowling around the complex, which has aerial cat doors and catwalks linking all or most of the apartments, including some that go from one floor to the next through the ceiling. In the condominiums, courtyards are redesigned with cats in mind—places where the felines congregate for sunshine, fresh air, tree climbing, and bird stalking. There are kitty litter compost heaps, and catnip and valerian herb beds.

Slightly shredded furniture is considered art, and of course there's the occasional cat fight—but it's all part of the charm.

EXAMPLE: SONGS OF SUNLIGHT CANARY PROVINCE

In this example, people in a condominium complex with a large central courtyard decide to create a Songs of Sunlight Canary Province. The Province Vision is to make its courtyard into a large aviary for canaries.

The central courtyard is redesigned with all manner of canary-friendly trees and shrubbery, where there is always a chorus of bird chatter and singing. Individual apartments that abut the central courtyard have bird doors and perches, where Sunshine and her friends can come and go, and interior aviaries for entertaining visitors.

Eventually the Songs of Sunlight Canary Province expands, connecting to wild canary provinces.

EXAMPLE: ENDLESS WATERS AQUARIUM PROVINCE

In this example, people in a warm, seaside region form an Endless Waters Aquarium Province. The Vision is to create and connect many outdoor and indoor aquariums, to form magnificent fish-ways.

Eventually, architects and aquatic specialists retrofit a succession of housing complexes with vast networks of interesting and unexpected waterways with waterfalls, connected ponds, water gardens, and aquariums.

No more little bowls and boring lives for Fishy.

Example: Fierce Falcon Province

In the old days, before the extensive enclosure of the land ruined falconry, the Greenland falcon was literally beyond price, being used with other of the great northern falcons, slight falcons, and sometimes the soft-feathered Easter Sacres, for flights at the kite, the Milan Royal, who in spite of his thieving and carrion-eating nature gave such sport that he was dignified with royal title.

—Ernest Lewis, Beth—A Sheep Dog

In this example, people create a Fierce Falcon Province with the Vision of reviving the sport of Falconry, once called "the sport of Kings."

Provincials with large, open tracts of land join to make the sport possible. Falcons and hawks of all hunting varieties are included in the Province.

Eventually, nature preserves and other parklands join the Province, adding to the extensive open lands.

The Province also forms Complementary relationships with Medieval and other Historic and Heritage Culture Provinces that feature falconry in their heritage.

ENERGY PROVINCES

Vintage street scene with gas lamps, by Ontsunan, stock.adobe.com

The homes, businesses, and travelways of all creative provinces will employ various types of energy. But some provinces will be created with the Primary Vision of promoting a particular type of energy, or a way to use energy.

A creative province energy vision might include a particular source of energy, such as electricity; a particular way to produce energy, such as an off-grid solar-powered system; or a particular way to use energy, by specifying such things as its type of lighting, hours of lighting, type of furnaces, or the types of stoves and ovens.

It is important to consider that localized sources of energy can be made to be very stable, secure, and sustainable compared to larger grid systems. Secondly, they can be used in conjunction with larger grid systems, with one or the other being backup systems. Thirdly, the energy from such localized systems can be rented to larger grid systems for added income.

EXAMPLE: FIRESIDE PROVINCE

In this example, a Fireside Province is formed in a heavily forested region with the Vision of sustainably using wood for heating and cooking. The Province has many provincials located in remote, wooded areas, as well as hubs that have formed in more heavily populated areas where there are wood-fueled power plants.

As it grows, the Fireside Province includes a provincial industry of sustainable forestry, and the manufacturing of state-of-the-art wood furnaces and wood stoves.

The Province gradually builds its own provincial culture that includes woodland activities and arts, particularly wood carvings; and it draws on the likes of Paul Bunyan and other woodland legends. If you've ever cooked on a wood stove, you know they produce the most delicious foods, and this province is known for its exemplary cuisine. Fireside chats and campfires are favorite provincial social activities.

Example: T.S. Eliott Gaslight Province

Provincials will not have to recreate a period in history to have the enchantment of gas-lit homes or gas street lamps. Gas provinces could be formed with the vision of using local gas energy sources.

In this example, a T.S. Eliott Gaslight Province is entirely gas-powered, with a gas-powered local electric plant, and homes with gas lighting, gas fireplaces, gas heat, and gas cook stoves.

The most prominent cultural features of the T.S. Eliott Province are its beautiful and romantic displays of gas street lamps, horse-drawn carriages, and T.S. Eliott-inspired poetry.

Example: Zap-Safe ElecTrionic Province

At the time of this writing, the young wireless industry is using health- and environment-damaging microwave frequencies for its products. But even wired devices and building wiring can emit health-damaging magnetic and electric frequencies if not done properly. The health effects from this state of affairs are catastrophic, yet most mainstream medical professionals are just beginning to become aware of them. Our education, when it comes to electronic safety, needs a gigantic update.

Since it often takes decades before government safety reforms are put in place, people in this example create a

Zap-Safe ElecTrionic Province. Their Vision is to require that provincials employ safe practices with three potentially dangerous electromagnetic fields: wireless microwave radiation, magnetic fields, and electric fields.

Thus, in the Zap-Safe ElecTrionic Province, provincials either ban wireless devices, or carefully monitor them to eliminate unsafe frequencies; they use safe wiring in their homes and businesses; and they research safe practices for all electric and electronic technologies.

Soon the Zap-Safe ElecTrionic Province becomes not only a safe haven, but also a center of electronic health research and knowledge.

IV. Cultural Provinces

Après l'Office à l'Eglise de la Ste-Trinité, 1900, Paris, France by Jean Béraud

By their very nature, Creative Provinces will have a culture of some sort: A historic period, a particular art or architecture, a particular type of costume or appearance, particular kinds of relationships, a particular economic system, or a particular set of mores, philosophies, and activities. But some will have a culture or cultural feature as their Primary Vision. It is these we will call "cultural provinces."

Thus, the definition of a Cultural Province:

> **Cultural Provinces** *are those with a primary vision to establish or re-establish a particular culture or cultural feature.*

Cultural Provinces will thus either focus on creating new cultures, or reviving historic or heritage cultures in full or in part.

Humanity's cultures are among its Great Treasures. Just like we want to preserve Earth's different species, so do we want to preserve Humanity's various cultures. To do so, it will not be enough to preserve their artifacts in museums, just as it is not enough to preserve stuffed animals in a museum. Artisanship and other skills, languages, manners, and knowledge—these cannot be properly preserved when left on the shelf or in books. Humanity has seen too many of these go to dust. Cultures must be kept alive to be preserved.

It will help to keep cultures alive if we realize that they do not have to be time-linear. Cultures can be preserved through the passage of time, and even long-lost cultures can be revived with careful research.

Up until now we have gone along with various negative thinkers who have told us that "things change and you can never go back." This is nonsense. There is no immutable law of the Universe that says "thou cannot maintain cultural traditions." We are creative beings. We can create any kind of culture we want, any time we want. If we want a Medieval Province, then we can create a Medieval Province. And I'm not talking "theme park." If we want a real Camelot, then a real Camelot we shall have!

HISTORIC AND HERITAGE CULTURE PROVINCES

Andante (Sonata of the Pyramids), Mikalojus Konstantinas Ciurlionis, 1909

Humanity's History and Heritage are among its most important Great Treasures that must be cherished and preserved. Particularly significant will be the restoration of the pinnacle cultures of a place and period.

Historic Provinces will be those that investigate, analyze, and preserve actual history. They will look at what went right and what went wrong in historic periods and events, and what were the conditions that caused certain historical directions.

Historic Provinces thus will likely house libraries and educational establishments specializing in their historic period or culture. They will also preserve historic buildings, museums, battlefields, and other physical treasures, and they will reenact, as well as investigate and critique, historic events. Historic provinces will also want to honor their historic personages.

Heritage Culture Provinces will be those that bring to life the best features of a culture, and creatively expand upon it. They will address such questions as: What went *right* with this culture? What did we love about it? What about it do we want to preserve?

Thus Heritage Culture Provinces will preserve a particular heritage culture by *living* it, by making it the culture of the creative province. Particularly significant will be:

- The provincial revival of the culture's costume, arts, architecture, and environments;
- The preservation of heritage systems of manners and mores in their critical role of guiding human behavior;
- The provincial revival of heritage languages, not only to speak, but to interpret and use once again, the texts, songs, and folklore of endangered and lost cultures;[4] and
- The provincial revival of the equally numerous heritage industries, crafts, and skills of those cultures.

Historic and Heritage Provinces will often combine, with Historic Provinces at the core of Heritage Provinces, as the keepers of the actual historic treasures, and Heritage Provinces living the best of their period's culture in their own creative way.

Many cities, towns, and regions have had a Pinnacle Culture, and Historic and Heritage Provinces will be particularly successful when they help to preserve and revive the particular pinnacle culture of a place by centrally locating there: the Ancient Roman Empire in Rome; Classical Greece in Athens; Renaissance Italy in Venice and Florence; the American Old South in Charleston, Savannah, and New Orleans; and so forth.

Heritage Provinces will want to look into their culture's historic problems, and explore alternatives to violence and subjugation, but in ways that keep the good aspects of the culture intact. And they will want to honor their forebears who suffered so that we all might learn.

---

4. According to linguists, of the 15,000 or so languages and dialects in existence 10,000 years ago, about 7,117 are still spoken today. Of these, 40 percent are endangered. Source: Ethnologue—Languages of the World. www.ethnologue.com

For example, Heritage Provinces might replace witch burnings, slavery, and serfdom with provincial customs that are non-violent, enjoyable, and fair to all, but which also honor the history in a meaningful way. They might engage in provincial warfare, but as war games. They might conduct duels, but in ways that are not fatal. They might maintain divisions of labor, but in ways that give everyone a fair chance at different positions.

Thus, provincials of Heritage Provinces, instead of reviving the past as a painful experience, will experience their cultures in their idyllic form, and from an enlightened perspective.

> *Example: The Garden of Eden*
>
> Antediluvian and Ancient Provinces will be recreations of Humanity's earliest civilizations, the historic ones ideally centrally located in their authentic regions.
>
> Such creative provinces might be centers of scholarship, studying the long-lost civilizations' anthropology and reviving their architecture, languages, customs, and other aspects of their culture to the extent known. Some antediluvian and ancient provinces will form around archeological digs. Still others, such as Atlantis, might need to be more whimsical than historic until such time as more is discovered about them.
>
> In this example, a Province of the Garden of Eden is begun with the Vision of creating an extensive and beautiful garden paradise, based on the Old Testament story of Humanity's beginnings. It collects in its membership a vast network of lush organic gardens, and garden restaurants of vegetarian, living-foods cuisine. It also forms ties with the Sitchin Antediluvian Research Province (see the example under Education and Research Provinces) and the Living Earth Raw Foods Province (see the example under Health Provinces).
>
> The Garden of Eden is run by Adam and Eve, which are honorary roles awarded periodically to premier organic gardeners and ecologists. And of course, that old Serpent, and the Tree of Knowledge, figure prominently.

Example: Pharaonic Egypt

Why not have Pharaohs! There is no reason why, in this democratic age, we shouldn't be able to have pharaohs.

In this example, that is exactly what a Province of Pharaonic Egypt has. And barges down the Nile! Provincial "slaves" are students and apprentices who have basic freedoms and rights, and who can work their way up from slave-apprentice to engineer to mathematician to pharaoh.

The Province becomes a center of scholarship for Egyptology, astronomy, astrology, and mathematics, not to mention the ancient hidden and lost sciences. Hieroglyphics are used in writing, and the ancient language is spoken to the degree known. The Province is also dedicated to the physical work of reviving the ancient building techniques, as well as historic preservation and excavation, with long-term visions of building a modern pyramid.

The Province also re-enacts ancient events, and creates appropriate new cultural activities. The role of Pharaoh is an annual title given to the premier Egyptologist, mathematician, engineer, astrologer, or astronomer.

Cats, of course, are demigods.

Example: The Roman Empire

Think of it: Reviving the ancient republic!

In this example, the Roman Empire is indeed revived. A new line of Caesars and a Senate run the Province. Latin is spoken, period costume is worn, and ancient Roman history and culture are studied. The Province has Roman baths and other period amenities, and it holds chariot races, and a less bloody version of gladiator contests.

Since war was one of the main activities of the Age of Aires, and most particularly of Rome, the Province builds a provincial army and conducts war games with various other ancient provinces, such as Classical and Hellenistic Greece, Pharaonic Egypt, and Gaul, the winners taking certain losers as "slaves" for a period of time—but all in provincial fun, and the "slaves" have certain perks.

> EXAMPLE: CAMELOT

The Middle Ages are generally considered to have begun after the fall of the western Roman Empire in the Fifth Century, and merged into the European Renaissance in the Fifteenth Century. It includes the Byzantine period beginning in the Fifth Century, characterized by its architectural arches and domes; the Viking cultures; and the glorious Chivalric period.

Such provinces will be ideally centered in places where there are medieval cathedrals, monasteries, nunneries and abbeys, mosques and harems, in restored walled towns, and in areas around existing medieval castles.

Heritage Provinces of the Middle Ages will combine well with medieval-themed mythical and fantasy provinces, such as Middle Earth.[5]

In this example, Humanity's greatest mythical medieval society, Camelot, is created as an amalgam of the Chivalric world, and eventually becomes the center of a Medieval Province Federation, which includes such glorious walled towns as Carcassonne, France; Avila, Spain; Taroudant, Morocco; and Pingyao, China.

Here the rich tapestry of Chivalric culture is preserved as a living province. Camelot decides to run itself with both a Knights of the Round Table, and a Ladies of the Round Table, each chosen annually in a glorious tournament. King Arthur and Queen Guinevere are then selected and crowned in a cathedral ceremony, for there is also a vibrant high-Church culture; and monasteries, outlawed in England by Henry VIII, are revived here in the Medieval provincial world.

In an adjacent Province of Norman England, the war between King Stephen and Empress Maud is being fought, and in a monastery in Shrewsbury, Brother Cadfael[6] is poking around investigating mysteries using his prodigious knowledge of herbs. Of course the herbs in this and all such creative provinces retain their medieval names, which help

---

5. From J. R. R. Tolkein's *The Hobbit* and other works.
6. From the mysteries of Ellis Peters.

identify their natural use, such as Knight's Milfoil, the herb that stanches bleeding.

Elsewhere in England the Wars of the Roses are ongoing between the Medieval Provinces of Lancaster and York, and in other creative provinces in England and France the Hundred Years War is ongoing, and Henry's archers are reviving the longbow at Agincourt.

Example: God of Thunder Viking Province

Also among the Medieval Provinces, we might have this example: a God of Thunder Viking Province, formed to revive the Viking culture, at its pinnacle in Scandinavia from the Eighth to Tenth Centuries.

The Province Vision is to be a collection of Norse communities who live the Viking traditions. Most of these are seafaring communities, with rebuilt and working Viking ships and fishing vessels. Provincials speak various medieval dialects of the Old Norse languages and practice Norse religions and customs.

The Province has its settlements of longhouses, and also builds a Viking-themed castle where it holds its ceremonies, with great banquets of fish and wild game, and the sloshing of mead and ale from horns and tankards.

The Province has decided to embellish its culture with the music of Nordic composers whose majestic music and themes reach back to this period. Wagnerian operas in particular, are borrowed from a later period, and performed.

The Province culture includes war games, with occasional Viking attacks on other creative provinces. When heroic Viking warriors die they are honored in Viking funerals on burning boats, sending the dead heroes off to Valhalla.

Provincial industries develop that include fishing, mead and ale brewing, sword making, and ship building, all reviving heritage skills and craftsmanship.

Example: Renaissance Venice

The Renaissance will be a favorite era of Historic and Heritage Culture Provinces, by nature of its expansiveness and creative beauty. The Renaissance saw the flowering of literature, intellectual pursuits, manners, visual arts, and costume—unparalleled anywhere else in human history. Probably the most appropriate symbol of this cultural pinnacle were the plumed hats worn by men of distinction.

The divinely inspired cathedral construction of the period can arguably be considered the pinnacle of architectural beauty and craftsmanship.

And perhaps the place that exemplified this magnificent era most of all was the Republic of Venice. In this example, Venetians form a Province of Renaissance Venice, to restore, preserve, and enhance this pinnacle culture. Using Venice's exquisite architecture and art as its backdrop, the Province revives the customs and costumes of the period, rebuilds its breathtaking tall ships, and becomes a new center of provincial Venetian trade.

Example: Province of Colonial and Revolutionary-Era America

When we think of the Georgian period, certainly the novels of Jane Austen come to mind, as well as powdered wigs, elaborate gowns, and a high society marked by salons and balls. Political change was also on the menu, with Jacobite risings, the American and French Revolutions, and the Napoleonic Wars. Georgian Provinces will want to embrace the exemplary costume, impeccable manners, and breathtaking political movements of this era, and might be centered in and around Georgian-period villages as backdrops for their revival.

In this example, a Colonial and Revolutionary America Province is formed in and around numerous Eastern American towns where there are an abundance of preserved colonial buildings and artifacts, and active historical societies. Places such as Concord, Massachusetts, and Charlottesville, Virginia, home of Jefferson's Monticello, become great centers of this Historic and Heritage Province.

Period costume is worn throughout the Province, and the language, manners, and other period traditions are embraced. Province areas are closed to modern technologies, with garages and lockers available around their perimeters, where provincials and visitors can park cars, change into period clothing, and be picked up by horse-drawn coaches, or perhaps travel by bateau down a stream to a destination.

A viable provincial industry develops, as period fashion designers, tailors, blacksmiths, stables, veterinarians, period newspapers, and town criers establish shops and businesses throughout the Province. Farming in the Province is done in the old tradition, including utilizing work horses.

The provincial culture includes such things as reenactments and investigations of Colonial and Revolutionary historical events, and new heritage-appropriate activities such as balls and town meetings.

EXAMPLE: VICTORIAN PROVINCE

In this example, people form a Victorian Province, a Historic and Heritage Province that meanders throughout England, in Victorian sections of London and other British cities and towns, as well as in India and other significant colonial locations. As these Province enclaves grow, they are able to replace automobiles and other modern technologies with their more charming predecessors.

Certain Victorian-era personages and institutions, real and fictional, come to life here, such as Sherlock Holmes and Old Scotland Yard, as well as characters from the works of Charles Dickens, Anthony Trollop, Thomas Hardy, and the Brontë sisters. Ghandi, Mountbatten, and the Queen herself, as well as other historical characters, become honorary figures in the Province.

The provincial culture is decidedly lacey and melodramatic, with impeccable manners, courtship rituals, and the language of flowers. Old brick streets are uncovered, gas street lamps are revived, and the Province is filled with horse drawn cabs, and Bobbies who keep things in order. Men in top hats, waistcoats, and gloves frequent their clubs where they discuss issues over cigars, brandy, and cards. Ladies in corsets, layers of petticoats, and elaborately embroidered gowns, with décolletage and lace gloves and fans preside over recitals, tableaus, and the occasional séance.

Example: Province of The Old South

In this example, a Province of The Old South is formed in the American Deep South as a comprehensive Historic and Heritage Province of the antebellum period through the Civil War and Reconstruction periods.

The Historic Province collects in its membership many Civil War battlefield parks, historical societies, museums, and historic buildings. Province Historic activities include the study and reenactment of battles and other significant events of the period, and historic personages are revived as honorary positions.

Provincial hubs form in the preserved sections of cities such as Charleston and Savannah. Provincials recreate plantation society, this time with small, family farmsteads centered around gracious mansions where cultural activities are held.

The Heritage Province maintains the culture of the period by following Nineteenth Century manners and costume, and by engaging in heritage activities such as grand balls, picnics, and society teas.

But all this provincial activity is now done with an enlightened modern perspective, which might include, among other things, plantations run as farm cooperatives, and African descendants living the life of a plantation master and similar positions in society. Thus the Province becomes a shining example of reviving what was good about a pinnacle culture and period, relegating its bad aspects to historical study, and reviving customs in a way that honors our antecedents who suffered so that we might learn.

The Old South is in many places a horse and period train and waterways province, with Province Horse Roads connecting province areas, an active Lincoln-Davis Train Line (see this example in the Transportation Provinces section), and a growing fleet of period ships and shipyards.

The Old South Province also becomes a parent province, and eventually a province federation, for many smaller creative provinces, such as a Brer Rabbit Heritage Province, an American Civil War Era Province, a Lincoln-Davis Train Line, a Mississippi River Heritage Province, and Old New Orleans.

EXAMPLE: BRER RABBIT HERITAGE PROVINCE

Proto-creative-province intentional communities, such as Oyotunji in South Carolina, offer an African-American heritage-preserving alternative to the surrounding globalist non-culture.

In our example, a Brer Rabbit Heritage Province is formed with the Vision of studying, reviving, and preserving early African-American culture and industries, and using the whimsical folk tales of Brer Rabbit and his animal friends for its artistic and environmental backdrop.

The Uncle Remus stories, as chronicled by Joel Chandler Harris, represent the largest single collection of African-American folktales ever published. Harris collected hundreds of folktales from many southern African American communities in the late 1800s, chronicling their dialects as closely as possible.

Julius Lester later updated many of the stories to make their language more accessible to the modern reader, publishing *The Tales of Uncle Remus: The Adventures of Brer Rabbit*,[7] which is wonderfully illustrated by Jerry Pinkney with whimsical paintings of the old countryside. These paintings and stories all become the inspiration for the rural setting of the Province.

To revive the early African-American culture, provincials study and speak the early dialects, which aid in the study of family archives and stories; and it uses the folklore, as well as films and other art, for its inspiration.

As the Province collects members and properties, hubs form where provincials restore small farm communities and revive the heritage arts, architecture, and cottage industries of the Nineteenth Century American South. Storytellers abound in the Province, and Brer Rabbit, Brer Fox, and other animals from the folktales populate its quaint countryside.

---

7. *The Tales of Uncle Remus: The Adventures of Brer Rabbit,* as told by Julius Lester, illustrated by Jerry Pinkney, Dial Books, New York, 1987.

Example: Zane Gray Wild West Province

In this example, a Zane Gray Wild West Province revives the Old American West in all its wild glory. It is most decidedly a horse and period-train province, with restored and replicated Nineteenth-Century trains and horse-drawn stagecoaches and horse-, mule- and oxen-drawn wagon trains. There are cowboys and cattle drives, campfires and cowboy songs with guitar strumming, and wild-horse roundups.

Province hubs form in towns where period buildings have been restored, and the Province boasts its dance halls and saloons with their piano music and period costume.

Famed ranches—fictional and historic—are brought to life as real working ranches, which have Province participating-visitors instead of tourists.

There are also the occasional provincial deviants—cattle rustlers and other outlaws. The Province is run by provincial mayors and sheriffs, who keep things under control, and insist on gunfights being done with blanks. Or whatever.

Example: The Sioux Nation Heritage Province

Indigenous peoples can form creative provinces to revive and protect their cultures, and to create their own protected regions beyond government-imposed reservation boundaries.

While today's modern sentiment is to protect indigenous tribes, nevertheless, many tribes, particularly those in rich rainforest regions, are still being decimated. Their land is being stolen and ecologically destroyed—actions driven for the most part by corporate greed. One way to help fend off this tide is to form creative provinces.

In this example, a Sioux Nation Heritage Province is formed with the Vision of reviving the Sioux Nation to its pinnacle culture—the pre-industrial society where its tribes lived a migratory and nature-centered life of hunting and gathering, and honoring the Earth.

In the Sioux Nation Heritage Province, provincials ride horses, usually bareback, hunt deer and buffalo with bow and arrow, revive migratory gathering traditions, live in teepees, make and wear traditional costume, speak the Sioux language, and engage in pow-wows and other heritage traditions.

The Province develops an enormously successful provincial visitation industry, which includes teaching visitors Earth-centered healing and spirituality, and Earth-respecting hunting and gathering.

The Sioux Nation Heritage Province also participates in provincial activities with many other creative provinces, such as historic battle reenactments with the Zane Gray Wild West Province.

EXAMPLE: RUSTIC HAWAII

In this example, people recreate the heritage culture of pre-industrial-era Hawaii, forming a Province of Rustic Hawaii, and assiduously keep out modern cultural features.

The Vision of Rustic Hawaii is to restore the heritage culture, and the rustic environment, industries, and travel of the islands. The heritage royal families are restored to run the Province; the grass skirts and other features of the heritage fashion are worn; and the island language, music, cuisine, and travel by various single- and double-canoes are revived, as are other aspects of the slow life that made this paradise so exotic.

EXAMPLE: GREAT GATSBY PROVINCE

Many late Nineteenth Century and early Twentieth Century Provinces will be experimented with, as the artifacts of these cultures are still widely available to use in provincial reconstruction.

In this example, a Great Gatsby Province is formed as a revival of the Roaring 20's—also called "The Jazz Age." Its many hubs include the Art Deco district along Miami's South Beach, many sections of New York City, and similar enclaves throughout the Americas, Europe, the Mediterranean, and elsewhere.

The Province draws inspiration from the many creative works of the period, including its signature work, Fitzgerald's *The Great Gatsby*.[8] Others include the "Mapp and Lucia" series of novels by E. F. Benson,[9] the works of Ernest Hemmingway, and the stylish Philo Vance mysteries of S.S. Van Dine. Provincials wear 1920s fashions, go on treasure hunts, and attend Art Deco nightclubs and Speakeasies, where they dance the Charleston.

The Province also boasts many collections of restored and replicated early-model cars, and joins with the Great Gatsby Antique Automobile Province (see the example in the Motor Vehicle Provinces section).

Provincial industries soon develop throughout the Province, including period fashion designers, early-model automobile builders and restorers, and 1920s heritage restaurants and hotels.

> EXAMPLE: 1950S-ERA CULTURAL PROVINCE
>
> Many towns have preserved structures and artifacts of the 1950s, a time of expansion and building, not to mention the Baby Boom. In this example, a 1950s-Era Cultural Province is started in just such a town. The era was defined by the small and disconnected suburban families, or "nuclear families," that emerged in this automobile- and television-centered culture. Its culture was filled with chic fashion, nascent television shows, swank nightclubs, coffee houses and Beatniks, as well as the romantic music of such singers as Perry Como and Harry Bellefonte.
>
> The Province membership includes small businesses from the era, and nightclubs like the Copacabana make a big comeback, where the fashion is decidedly soigné. Other businesses include drive-in movie theatres and big-house theatres featuring such romantic icons as Doris Day and Rock Hudson, as well as Film Noir. There are restored soda fountains and cafés with juke boxes featuring Elvis and the various melodramatic teen love songs of the period. And provincials dance to music played on their record players and watch TV on cabinet televisions. Of course the Province

---

8. *The Great Gatsby*, F. Scott Fitzgerald.
9. *Queen Lucia* (1920) and other novels, E. F. Bensen.

boasts its own radio and television stations, as well as its own recording studios, with which they make new renditions of music and films based on the culture.

Many 1950s auto clubs and vintage appliance sellers join the Province, and period automobile and appliance restoration and replica industries develop.

The Province has federation relationships with Aunt Bea's Kitchen Garden Province (see this example under Farm and Cottage Industry Provinces), the Life of Riley Province (described in the Cultural Concept and Fantasy Provinces section), and "Old Hollywood."

Cultural-Concept and Fantasy Provinces

Guardian, © Betty Ann Fraley

Possibly the most interesting of all creative provinces will come under the category of Cultural-Concept and Fantasy Provinces. Here imagination can really stretch through provincial creativity.

In Cultural-Concept Provinces, any kind of cultural features, such as costume, physical appearance, activities, attitudes, behaviors, or ways of communicating, can be the essence of the Province's Vision.

In Fantasy Provinces, the visions of fantasy writers and artists will provide a wealth of ideas for truly magical ways to live. Such provinces can take form as Other Worlds of breathtaking beauty, delight, and awe. From the Munchkin's Land of Oz, to Tarzan's African Jungle, to Robin Hood's Sherwood Forest, and on to the moonlit desertscapes of sci-fi worlds, provincials will be able to bring to life the most enchanting and interesting communities of their imaginations.

Example: The Province of the Angels

A creative province can begin with the inspiration of a particular place's "Name of Destiny," described in Part III of this book.

In this example, people form a Province of the Angels in and around the city of Los Angeles, with the Vision of creating a true "City of Angels," with angelic arts, charitable endeavors, and "portal" activities for birth and death transitions and communications with the spiritual realm.

The arts in the Province of the Angels include angel statuary, murals, paintings, and other visual expressions of the heavenly realm. Fashion is decidedly angelic. Music is also angelic, featuring, among other things, harps, New Age compositions, and choirs dressed in gossamer robes.

To manifest the Province's Vision to be a place of charitable activities, charitable organizations are encouraged to join the Province, and provincial activities for peace, love, and assistance reach around the globe.

As a Portal Province, many provincials specialize in birthing and end-of-physical-life transitions, as well as communications with the Spirit Realm. (For more on portal provinces, see the Relationships and Life Stages Provinces section.)

Example: Life of Riley Province

In this example, people in an old neighborhood form a Life of Riley Province. Its Vision is to revive the laid-back neighborhood of yesteryear, with quiet streets; clean water; food prepared from scratch; children and pets running freely; clothes drying on the line; kitchen gardens; small lawns mowed with manual mowers; and of course the Province's signature hammock in every back yard.

The Province is run like a neighborhood association, headed by a periodically chosen "Riley."

Example: The Spoken Word Province

Two-dimensional written materials, while an enormous intellectual aid to Humanity, can also distract us from paying attention to *real-life* three-dimensional activity. Over time we have also tended to rely more and more on the written word, and less on verbal communication. Video and audio communications similarly distract us from real life.

Thus creative provinces where certain two-dimensional communications are restricted in certain ways can promote real-life activities, and can also promote alternative types of communication.

In this example, a Spoken Word Province is formed with the Vision that verbal communication is used as much as possible: Storytellers replace books, children learn to memorize and recite things verbally, announcers replace printed programs, and traveling minstrels and town criers report the news.

At least two interesting things happen in this Province: First, the provincials revive the skill of memorization; and secondly, they become highly skilled actors and orators.

Example: The Strange Province

In attitude provinces, things can start to get a bit bizarre, but certainly interesting. Possibilities include Happy, Cheerful, Cool, Silly, Funny, or Melodramatic. I would recommend staying away from Sad, Miserable, and Angry; however, a Boring Province might be just the cup of tea for some people.

In this example, a small group of people forms The Strange Province as a lark, and no one is more surprised than they, when the Province takes off and becomes enormously popular.

The Province Vision is that you have to be strange in some way, or your abode needs to be strange, to belong. Provincials do odd things, like walk backwards, wear weird clothing, and have peculiar houses and gardens. Surreal and quirky paintings, such as the works of Salvador Dalí and

Cultural-Concept and Fantasy Provinces | 153

Product of the Environment, © Walter Gurbo

Walter Gurbo, adorn interior landscapes. Streets meander to unexpected places. Plays have surprising endings. There are bizarre Province traditions. People have unusual pets.

Oddly, but perhaps not surprisingly, some very interesting new ideas come from this Province.

EXAMPLE: MIDDLE EARTH

In this example, a Province of Middle Earth takes its inspiration from *The Hobbit* and other works of J. R. R. Tolkein. The Province has properties nestled in several relatively wild and green hilly regions where provincial Hobbits, Goblins, and assorted other creatures live in huts and other primitive abodes. It also has an outpost, "The Edge of Doom."

The Province of Middle Earth eventually joins the Federation of Old Europe, which also includes such places as Camelot, the Celtic Province, the Druid Province, and the Province of Faerie.

EXAMPLE: PROVINCE OF FAERIE

In this example, fairy enthusiasts form a Province of Faerie. Their vision is to create a real world of fairies, the mythical creatures of multiple European cultures. The Province includes in its membership many faerie artists, doll-makers, and clothing designers. Leprechauns, gnomes, goblins, and other magical beings feature prominently.

The Province is begun in Ireland and has its headquarters there. But faerie enthusiasts are everywhere, and soon the province has a plethora of Fair Folk outposts.

Provincial industries develop that include faerie fashions, designs, dolls, and art books.

Example: The Jolly Roger Province

Because creative provinces are not limited by location, they can be mobile, moving around in gypsy caravans, houseboats, and space stations, to name several possibilities.

In this example, various pirate groups from the Society of Creative Anachronism form The Jolly Roger Province. Its vision is to revive the swashbuckling shipboard life depicted in Robert Louis Stevenson's *Treasure Island* and other historic and fictional accounts.

As the Province grows, it draws into its membership a fleet of corsairs—period pirate tall ships and smaller vessels.

The Jolly Roger Province eventually joins federations of Seventeenth, Eighteenth, and Nineteenth Century Historic and Heritage Provinces, engaging in periodic attacks upon their period vessels.

Example: Shangri-La

In this example, a Province of Shangri-la is started in a remote mountainous area, such as Tibet, to bring to life the legendary fictional Himalayan utopia created in the novel *Lost Horizon*, by James Hilton, and Frank Capra's film of the same title.

Shangri-La is run as a lamasery, and considers itself one of the seven sacred places of refuge for Buddhists during times of strife, spoken of in ancient Tibetan scriptures. Thus, while Shangri-la classifies itself as a fantasy province, its secondary vision is to embrace this Tibetan Buddhist spiritual tradition.

The Province also forms federation relationships with a number of resorts, hotels, and gardens from around the world that have patterned themselves after the Shangri-la story.

ARTISTIC AND ARCHITECTURAL CONCEPT PROVINCES

Treehouse, stock.adobe.com/Anabel

A creative province can have as its Primary Vision an Artistic or Architectural Concept. It can also have artistic and architectural concepts among its supporting visions, to enhance its provincial culture.

As with all aspects of provincial culture, let your province arts and architecture be a reflection of your Province Vision.

A creative province might feature a particular artist, architect, or a particular school or type of art or architecture. Some of the major categories to consider are:

- A kind of music or soundscape, such as Baroque music, choral music, church bells, or birdsong;
- A kind of dance, such as Scottish country dance, tango, samba, ballet, or dancing in the streets;
- A kind of visual art, such as watercolor painting, statuary, or topiary;
- A particular color palate, such as using color-coded buildings, doors, etc., to replace signs, or designating that architecture, costumes, and other visual expressions are a certain color;
- A kind of textile art, such as quilting, beadwork, or pottery;
- A type of written or dramatic art, such as Ancient Greek Tragedy, Beat poetry, or wandering minstrels;

- A kind of food, beverage, or cuisine, such as soul food, gourmet French cuisine, or local micro-brewed beers;
- A scentscape, such as old-variety flowers, a particular perfume, essential oils, or natural fresh air;
- A particular tactile feature, such as fur, velvet, or hard metals;
- A particular architecture or architectural concept, such as Scandinavian Stave churches, tiny houses, houseboats, geodesic dome/balloon houses for living and travel, or Medieval walled cities;
- A particular architectural element, such as gargoyles, murals, white picket fences, thatched roofs, or unusual doorways.

EXAMPLE: WINDS OF COLOR FLAG PROVINCE

Like other two-dimensional communications, billboards and other printed signs can distract one from paying attention to the *real, living* landscape or activity. There are many possible ways to replace signs, including using color-coded buildings, uniquely designed doors, or particular varieties of plants.

In this example, a breathtaking Winds of Color Flag Province is formed in an area where there is a good supply of sun and wind. The Province Vision is that flags are to be used instead of word-signs to designate places of business, streets, buildings, residences, and events. Flying flags and kites are also employed.

A provincial flag industry soon develops, as provincials design and make an endless variety of interesting and gorgeous flags. The Province becomes a landmark of beauty as flags and kites fly everywhere, bringing color to the wind.

EXAMPLE: KINCAID PROVINCE

The art of a particular artist can be a province vision, and this might be particularly desired in an area where the artist lived, or in a place that exemplifies his or her art, such as a Monet Province in Giverny, or a Strauss Waltz Province in Vienna.

In this example, a Kincaid Province is started in a village to enhance its quaint possibilities by featuring the villagescapes of the late artist Thomas Kincaid. Kincaid's idyllic scenes are recreated in the design of the village's cottages and landscape. The Province encourages and assists in the creation of vine-covered cottages, thatched and living-roof cottages, abundant flower gardens, and windows filled with golden light.

EXAMPLE: THE VELVET RABBIT PROVINCE

Provinces can be created to feature a certain artistic texture or feel. We might imagine, for example, a province where the artistic concept reflects the hardness of modernist architecture and design: metallic sculpture, modern furniture, hardedge modern art, and metallic colors.

In this example, a Velvet Rabbit Province is formed with the artistic vision of softness. The Province abounds in velvets, soft furry cats, geese, goose down pillows, soft meadows, birds' nests, and of course, rabbits, all of which run free. Nature, which is softness itself, is heavily featured in this Province, and another of its visions is to protect and revive its wild spaces and wildlife, such as its wild meadows and butterflies.

Another Province Vision is the humane and sustainable collection of fur, feathers, and other soft wild products, and a viable provincial industry develops of humanely produced natural clothing, soft toys, pillows, and decorative items.

EXAMPLE: VOICE OF HUMANITY CHORAL PROVINCE

In the current Western culture, most singing venues involve performers singing in front of an audience, church being the one big exception. But there is so much more we can do with song! We can sing as we work, at weddings, balls, parties, receptions, ceremonies, while we dine, and while we play.

In this example, a Voice of Humanity Choral Province is formed with the Vision of forming many choruses, and making them a major part of provincial life. Schools, clubs, and places of work all have their choruses, and provincials periodically stop their daily activities to sing. Barbers and hairdressers sing in their salons. In provincial restaurants, instead of piped-in music, waiters and waitresses, chefs and busboys serenade the diners, and diners sing between dinner courses. Choruses sing in the streets and at the market.

The province develops a viable industry hosting weddings and other rites-of-passage ceremonies. They sing such works as Puccini's "Humming Chorus" from *Madame Butterfly* at birthing ceremonies, Wagner's "Bridal Chorus" from *Lohengrin* at weddings, and the many Requiem Masses during Holy Week and at funerals.

Choral composers are drawn to the Province, and get their works sung in many provincial venues. The Province culture not only includes many small choral venues, but also great works performed by thousands of singers.

EXAMPLE: HERITAGE JAZZ PROVINCE

In this example, a group of preservation jazz musicians and night clubs form a Heritage Jazz Province, with the vision of creating a place where early jazz is preserved, and music is live and acoustic, rather than piped in or amplified. There are clubs that specialize in Blues, Ragtime, Dixieland, and many others. There is heritage dancing in most of the clubs, and depending on the type of jazz, provincials dance the Argentine tango, the samba, early African-American dance, and modern variations.

The Province grows as more jazz clubs and musicians join. Soon a province hub forms in a city neighborhood where people flock to the clubs to dance and share original jazz. The Province is instrumental in creating a Jazz Renaissance.

EXAMPLE: GRAND BALL PROVINCE

In this example, a Grand Ball Province is begun with the vision of featuring the Grand Ball, with stringed orchestras, ballrooms, elaborate costumes, and people who want to recreate the magnificent social-art of group dancing.

The Province has outposts in cities such as Vienna, where Waltzing Balls are featured. In other Province outposts, other dances are featured, such as Cotillions, Scottish Country Dance, Contra Dancing, Square Dancing, the Minuet, and the Polka. And some Province outposts feature entirely new group dance arts. The Grand Ball Province soon spreads, and one can literally dance oneself around the world.

The Province culture centers around these Grand Balls, with their orchestras, and provincials dressed in appropriate costume, such as men dressed in long coats and tails twirling ladies in elegant full-skirted gowns; cowboy attire at square dances; and Old German costume at polka dances.

Provincials also host Dance Socials, where the wondrous dances are taught in a slightly less formal social setting.

Example: Pretty Tiny House Province

A type of dwelling, such as such as tee-pees, mud huts, caravans, A-frames, igloos, or houseboats can be a defining feature of a creative province. A type of architecture or building material can also be featured.

In this example, people form a Pretty Tiny House Province with the vision of creating a community of small dwellings with aesthetically pleasing designs. Architects and builders join the Province, creating small dwellings of beauty and economy of space. The Pretty Tiny Houses are linked with footpaths through gardens, meadows, and woods.

The Province culture includes house building, and awards for the most beautiful, endearing, livable, and economical dwellings.

Example: Other Worlds Space City

In an example of a province with a larger design vision we have an Other Worlds Space City, started by people who are interested in creating a large community that is magnificent and other-worldly. They are located in an area where there is already a space port (such as the Star Trek Space Portal Province, described in the Air Transportation and Travelways section), as well as nearby scientific schools, industries, and an observatory.

The Province Vision is to bring together a comprehensive design of architecture and art that is other-worldly and space-age, and which will take creative shape over time, particularly to house the growing space travel activities. Provincials hold design competitions for artists and architects of all types, and a magnificent group creation develops.

Relationship and Life Stages Provinces

The Funeral of a Viking, Frank Dicksee, 1893

In this category we have creative provinces comprised of people with a primary vision of focusing on certain relationships, familial or friendship, or focusing on particular life stages and events.

Many creative provinces will also have such relationship and life stages customs among their supporting visions: events such as births, marriages, and funerals; and relationship customs such as courtship.

Example: Bright Dawn Birthing Province

What joy to be present where new lives are being born! And yet we've hardly begun to explore the endlessly magnificent ways to bring about the miraculous beginning of our physical lives. We can do so much more than begin lives in sterile hospitals with square walls and fluorescent lights.

The vision of the Bright Dawn Birthing Province is to be a place where birthing is offered in beautiful surroundings with memorable ceremonies. There are endless creative birthings: in lagoons filled with lotus flowers and people humming beautiful melodies; in meadows of wildflowers with grandmothers and aunts holding hands in laughter and joy; under the stars and moonlight, surrounded by a chorus of singing and dancing people; around bonfires with dancers and drumming; and among the natural quietude of birdsong at sunrise. Imagine being born into this new, wonderful world!

The Bright Dawn Birthing Province has many midwives and other birthing professionals in its membership, as well as gardeners, musicians, and choruses. A joyous culture of birth, flowers, and music develops.

Example: Amazon Matriarch Province

Some people might want to create provinces exclusive of their gender. Examples of such gender-specific creative provinces might include maternal clans, male-bonding provinces, and monastic provinces. Or a province might define itself as being androgynous, with provincials taking neither a male nor female identity, with the provincial fashion being decidedly neutral.

In this example, a group of women forms an Amazon Matriarch Province. Its Vision is to form matriarchal clans based on the ancient Mediterranean Amazonian culture, to the extent known, including reviving the ancient religion honoring the Goddess. As such, it is both a Historic and Heritage Culture Province and a Relationship and Life Stages Province.

The Amazon Matriarch Province follows a matrilineage, with girls taking their mother's names. Women and girls are trained in the ancient martial arts of the Age of Aires, and participate in occasional battles with Classical and Hellenistic Greece and other ancient warrior provinces.

Example: Larson Family Heritage Province

In this example, taken from the author's own family heritage, some of the descendents of John Alfred and Augusta, and later Maria (after Augusta's death) Larson, who established a farm in the late 1800s in Valley Springs, South Dakota, decide to go back there and buy properties to create a Larson

Family Heritage Province. At first, two or three descendents buy land, and later more arrive to join the Province.

The Province is mainly comprised of family farms run in the old tradition, with a variety of farm animals and crops, as well as various cottage industries.

The provincials return to the local church of their forebears, reestablish a Grange chapter, and in many other ways help to invigorate the local community and revive its heritage culture.

EXAMPLE: GRANDPARENTS ON ROLLER SKATES PROVINCE

Forming communities for one's generation is something retired people have done widely, and retirement communities in particular are one of the most successful types of proto-provinces. But by provincializing we can do much more with them.

In our example, a Grandparents on Roller Skates Province, people form a retirement community based on all manner of personal-wheeled transportation, such as scooters and go-carts. But they go a step further and make roller-skating its primary Vision—to give themselves a daring and fun activity: roller skating in many venues. They test their provincials to make sure all roller skaters have bones strong enough to withstand the occasional body crash.

The retirement community is thus transformed from ho-hum into a fun and surprising place, with elders on roller skates gliding around, waiting tables in a Province restaurant, holding roller skating dances, and zooming past their youngsters on the sidewalk and various unexpected places.

EXAMPLE: SUNSET VIGIL PROVINCE

There are as many ways to approach the end of physical life, as there are attitudes about death and the afterlife. As with birthing, we can do so much more than the sterile hospital setting.

Hospice, which endeavors to make physical death a gentle experience in the home, and the "Last Wishes" program, which finds ways to bring joy and closure to people before we bid them farewell, are steps in the right direction toward making our passing a good experience. But with End-of-Physical-Life Provinces, so much more can be done to embrace and honor people at this greatest-of-all transition.

Creative provinces that feature end-of-physical-life customs might have choral vigils to bid farewell to the departing spirits; they might have cruises through breathtaking fjords; they might engage in heroic battles; or they might offer a meditative environment in a garden, wilderness or Sacred Grove (see the St. Francis Sacred Grove example in the next section).

In this example, a Sunset Vigil Province is formed along a beautiful shore, where provincials have home-style inns and offer many vigils: a plethora of snuggling cats; birdsong meditations; and their signature sunset vigil with choruses of singing provincials, and glorious skyscapes.

What wonderful, loving ways to say goodbye to our lives on Earth as we enter the Spirit Realm.

Philosophical, Religious, and Spiritual Provinces

Two Buddhist Monks, AdobeStock

Historically, one of the primary reasons Humanity has fought over religion is because it has attempted to stipulate religious rules under the umbrella of the sovereign state, which, as discussed in Part One of this book, is not structured to handle them. The very nature of sovereign states is that they encompass, within their permanent borders, heterogeneous populations of all manner of opinions and lifestyles. Therefore proclamations insisting that all their citizens be of a particular religion or philosophy, not to mention lifestyle, are bound to create problems.

The genius of such documents as the American Bill of Rights is that they declare the divinely-given rights and freedoms of the citizenry, including that the sovereign state must be neutral and leave people to practice whatever religion they choose. The result is that Americans, for all their numerous and sundry religions and houses of worship, do not fight over religion.

But we must add to this the organic fact that people will want to live in communities with people of similar beliefs and lifestyles; hence the important role of intentional communities.

There are numerous religious proto-provinces that have developed organically. Religious communities that have dispersed around the globe have, over the centuries, connected with one another through houses of worship, many creating neighborhood hubs, such as the Orthodox Jewish communities. Monasteries and Convents are also a type of religious intentional community.

Creative provinces might also be extensions of houses of worship: un-boundaried communities following certain religious practices.

Thus, by provincializing, religious communities can expand their connections so that they form hubs for engaging in the spiritual life. Such creative provinces could be either allied with a specific religion, or be non-denominational and focused on a particular religious concept.

EXAMPLE: ST. FRANCIS PROVINCE AND SACRED GROVE

In this example, people form a creative province based on the humanitarian teachings of St. Francis of Assisi. It begins in an area that already has an active monastery and convent, and from there it expands in provincial hubs.

The Vision of the St. Francis Province is to live the Christian life, with particular emphasis on the teachings of St. Francis. The Province is devoted to helping people as well as wildlife and domestic animals, and includes a Sacred Grove. (See also the example, Easter Passion Sacred Grove in the Environmental Concept Provinces section.)

The St. Francis Sacred Grove combines orchards, as well as vineyards and gardens, to create sacred memorial grounds for both people and animals. It is very much a visiting province, with its provincial caretakers administering burials and memorials on land that has been permanently given over to the Province.

Instead of a headstone, a memorial might be a tree, shrub, or bank of flowers planted above or alongside a grave, with an inscription engraved on a plaque. Memorials also take the form of birdhouses, bat houses, wild bee houses, and other wildlife habitats.

Depending on the specific location, to visit your loved ones you walk, bicycle, or take a horse-drawn carriage. Fruit and nuts from the orchards are sold at various places by St. Francis provincials.

EXAMPLE: WISDOM CIRCLE PROVINCE

In this example, people create a Wisdom Circle Province as a community of wise people who give advice.

The Province is run by a Circle of Wise Ones, which meets regularly to hear, discuss, and give advice on all manner of issues: personal, local community, and worldly.

As the Province grows, concentric wisdom circles form in outlying Province hubs. There are Wisdom Circles of indigenous peoples, of various religious orders, Oracles of Classical Greece, and of scholars in the humanities and sciences, to name a few.

Economic Concept Provinces

Floating market in Mekong Delta, Vietnam, Phuong

> *Work and play are words used to describe the same thing under different conditions.*
> —Mark Twain

The world has been, for a long time, moving toward a huge, centralized, from-the-top-down economy, where a tiny group of people controls all aspects of it, from the top of a pyramid structure.

But creative provinces can help us to not only regain our localized economies, but to also create decentralized economies of every kind imaginable.

To accomplish this it is important that we follow the Universal Principle of Resonance: The more we consume "from the top down" products, such as foods from huge industrialized corporate farms, or products from faraway sweatshops whose serf-like practices are hidden behind complex trade agreements, the more we ourselves live in a huge, "from the top down," controlled society with little physical or economic freedom. Conversely, the more we consume locally produced, organic, and humanly raised products from both freely raised animals and from economically free people, the more we ourselves become free. (See more examples of resonance under Principle 2.)

Some people will choose to create a province vision based on an economic concept, such as a provincial currency, or a form of barter, or a culture of gifting, or the sharing of meals, either as their primary vision, or as a supporting vision.

Or a creative province might be formed around a shared workshop—a mechanical garage workshop, a sewing room, a greenhouse, laundry, or a community kitchen. These can become cultural centers of their respective creative provinces, where provincials not only help each other with projects, but also engage in socializing and other cultural activities.

Example: Patty Cake Cooperative Baking Province

In this example, a Patty Cake Cooperative Baking Province is created based around several church commercial kitchens. The provincials use the kitchens to bake their own breads and pastries, and to exchange recipes and gossip.

As the Province grows, it gathers into its membership several hand grain mills, as well as a large old grain mill, which it restores and uses. Eventually, Patty Cake grows to become an Industry Province, developing its own viable baking industry, and selling its baking products in the region.

Example: Elegant Dinners Province

Dining Provinces can be formed where people want to have shared meals of some type. Many variations of this model are possible, such as creative provinces where provincials share a certain number of their meals at local restaurants; or where provincials have regular shared dinners in a church hall.

Shared dinner province visions can also work well in creative provinces that want to promote a certain type of cuisine, such as organic, raw, or gourmet.

In this example, an Elegant Dinners Province is formed with the Vision of regular shared formal dinners, where provincials dress for dinner and have formal table settings with candlelight, and a particular refined entertainment feature. The dining venues start in provincials' homes, and as the Province expands, many more dining venues are added.

Example: Pound of Flesh Province

Creative provinces can devise their own provincial methods of exchange that are valid only in the Province. For example, Historic and Heritage Provinces might use period money, such as Confederate dollars, Roman coins, and the like. The nice thing about such a tiered system of money is that it offers a level of exchange that is more personal, like bartering and gifting, where people can exchange goods and services with people they know and care about, in a way they see as fair and friendly. And in provincial exchange, we have the opportunity to require a fair exchange in the most creative of ways.

In this example, a tongue-in-cheek-named Pound of Flesh Province has a Vision to create an elaborate barter system of trading goods and services, with a Provincial Court to settle any differences. Using a spreadsheet, provincials track exchanges. Thus, Ethelred trades a half day of his carpentry services per week, for two loaves of Matilda's bread, six eggs, and a cup of churned butter. And if Ethelred reneges on his promise to include a window in the outhouse he's built for Mortimer, after Mortimer so kindly made him a suit of armor, he is brought before Portia, the judge, who requires him to not only cut a window in the outhouse, but to add a glass pane as well!

EXAMPLE: BRIGADOON BIODYNAMIC SELF-SUSTAINING PROVINCE

One ambitious type of creative province would be a self-sustaining province, where the provincials grow and manufacture much of what they use, such as food, housing, power, transportation, clothing, and cultural activities, and become increasingly self-sufficient. Such creative provinces could have sustainability in varying degrees as a primary or supporting vision.

In this example, people who live in a lush valley with many food and energy resources, recreate Brigadoon, inspired by both the culture depicted in the classic musical by Alan Jay Lerner and Frederick Loewe, and by the bio-dynamic farming philosophy of Rudolf Steiner.

"The 'true farm,' in biodynamic terms, lives and works as a single organism, supporting itself in all its functions and requiring outside help only as a temporary remedy."[10]

The vision of Brigadoon is to become increasingly self-sufficient, based on biodynamic principles, and to adopt a rather insular culture based on the various legends of disappearing villages from countries around Old Europe, such as the mythical German village of Germelshausen, from a story by Friedrich Gerstacker. In the story of Brigadoon, the magical Scottish Highlands village appears to outsiders for only one day every one hundred years.

The Brigadoon Biodynamic Self-Sustaining Province decides to not be quite so insular, and as part of its culture, hosts visitors on a regular basis, to teach them biodynamic farming, but with the stipulation that they not reveal Brigadoon's magic.

---

10. From *The Encyclopedia of Organic Gardening,* by the staff of *Organic Gardening* magazine, Rodale Press, 1978.

PART 3
FIVE STEPS TO BUILDING A CREATIVE PROVINCE

Wisdom Builds Her House (Proverbs 9: 1-6), collage by Jane Evelynne Higgins (1959 - 2019), courtesy of Timothy Main

I. **Create Your Primary Vision** / 173
II. **Create Supporting Visions to Further Shape Your Province** / 179
III. **Create Rules To Protect Your Vision** / 202
IV. **Accumulate and Chronicle Your Heritage Treasures** / 211
V. **Activate Your Province with Real, Live Activities** / 222

Introduction to Part 3

Bringing Your Vision To Life

Whatever you think you can do or believe you can do, begin it. Action has magic, grace, and power in it.

—Johann Wolfgang von Goethe

It is now time for you to form a Creative Province, and for you and your fellow provincials to activate its real Provincial Life. In Part 3 we take you through the initial steps to create your province's Vision and its Visionary System, and to accumulate and activate the Heritage Treasures that will make your Vision a reality.

In creating your provincial life, there are three themes to always keep in mind:

The first major theme of Provincial Life is **to engage in real activities.** Recall Principle 2: Creative Provinces are "the Real Thing" rather than "the appearance of." They are real places where people live, work, and travel. Provincials are *doing* things rather than watching someone else do them. However, to learn to do their many activities, provincials will of course obtain guidance, including from films and books.

A second theme of Provincial Life is **to enjoyably manage the Province.** That means managing the Province in appropriately fun ways to manifest its Vision. If your Province activity is not enjoyable, that is a flashing sign that you are not doing it right!

A third theme of Provincial Life is **to meaningfully and appropriately use the Province's Heritage Treasures**. This means using the skills and other resources you together possess in ways that best manifest the province vision and build the community as a magnificent art form.

I. Create Your Primary Vision

Eagle Bridge Hotel, Grandma Moses

The Primary Vision is the most important and constant defining characteristic of a Creative Province. While any supporting visions the province develops might change with time, the Primary Vision is what remains constant and intact. With this in mind, the following are five principles for creating your Primary Vision:

1. Create the Primary Vision as an Active, Real Place for Living, Working, and/or Traveling

Creative Provinces are real places where people live, work, and travel. Thus, the Primary Province Vision must be *active* in nature. We are creating real, active, three-dimensional places of wonder and enchantment in which to spend our time. We are making our dreams come alive.

> EXAMPLE: THE PRIMARY VISION OF THE NORTH POLE: "A TOYMAKING PROVINCE OF SANTA CLAUS"
>
> The Primary Vision of a North Pole Province might be: "A Creative Province where real toymakers, mostly of diminutive size, and a Santa Claus of large girth and full white beard, physically live and work, and manage the Province and its toy distribution network, and who also care for a herd or reindeer, in a northern region of the globe, following the ancient winter-festival and gift-giving cultural traditions of Yule, Christmas, Hanukah, and many others."

2. CREATE THE PRIMARY VISION AS A POSITIVE GOAL OF WHAT YOU WANT TO CREATE

It has been proven time and again that focusing on what you *want*, (rather than on what you *don't want*), is the most powerful way to create. Thus it is vital that you state your Province Primary Vision as a *positive* goal.

State exactly what you *want* to create, which is a powerful statement of vision. Do not phrase your vision as something you *don't* want, which would instead give focus and power to what you don't want.

> EXAMPLE: GRANDFATHER RIVER RESTORATION PROVINCE
>
> In this example, a Grandfather River Restoration Province might state its Primary Vision as: "A Creative Province for the local ecological, industrial, travel, and cultural restoration of the Grandfather River environs." This is a positive vision that focuses on and gives strength to what the creators *want*.
>
> Conversely, stating the Primary Vision as "The removal of pollution, and river-destroying dams from the Grandfather River" would give too much focus and strength to what the creators did *not* want. These sorts of specifics can

instead be stated in Supporting Visions, but even then they should be carefully worded as positive goals. For example, "The restoration of river-flow and fish migration through such things as the careful removal of obsolete and destructive dams."

3. CREATE THE PRIMARY VISION WITH SPECIFIC AND SUCCINCT LANGUAGE

Be very specific and succinct in stating your Primary Vision. If you are too general and vague, you will invite all manner of activities that you do not want.

EXAMPLE: GOD'S FIELDS PROVINCE

For example, a specific and succinct Primary Vision for a God's Fields Province might be "A Province of small and independently-owned farms using sustainable horticulture practices." Such a province would encourage the bringing back of heritage varieties of grains and other plants, as well as encourage the revitalization of depleted soil and local economies.

On the other hand, if the Province's Primary Vision was vaguely worded as "A Province of farms," then it would invite all manner of practices that are destructive to the environment, health, and local economies that we are seeing today in corporate agriculture.

4. CREATE THE PRIMARY VISION AS SOMETHING TO BENEFIT THE WORLD

Creative provinces can be formed with almost any vision in mind—there is no limit to human creativity. But one built with a vision that benefits the world, and creates a wonderful place where people want to live, work, and travel, probably will be very successful and long-lived.

Conversely, creative provinces built on selfish visions are doomed to failure. Selfish province visions include those that are unethical, illegal, inhumane, destructive to the environment, destructive to local economies, annoying to neighbors, or which encourage strife.

For example, if you created a province that was based on an activity that polluted the environment (with noise or chemicals, for example), your surrounding communities would probably organize to pass zoning or other laws to prevent your activities. So why devote your precious time, energies, and other resources to creating a province that is doomed to failure?

Always keep in mind that you are creating places where people will want to *live, work,* and *travel.*

| EXAMPLE: THE OLD SOUTH

> Historic and Heritage Provinces will, in a variety of ways, deal with old conflicts. Thus, they will need to be sensitive to those issues, and head off strife at the outset by stating their visions in a beneficial way.
>
> In this example, the primary vision of a Province of The Old South might be "To Revive the Cultures, Travelways, Environments, and Industries of the Southern Colonies of the United States of the Eighteenth and Nineteenth Centuries in Ways That Are Egalitarian and Sustainable." This vision would encourage all manner of beautiful, fun, and industrious period activities, in ways that replaced the historic slavery-centered economy with independent farms and other local industries. Such a creative province would probably be very successful.
>
> On the other hand, if the Province's vision statement was vaguely worded "To revitalize the historic culture of the Old South," it could be perceived as being open to reviving the historic racially divisive practices, which would invite criticism and lead to failure.
>
> Thus, if you create a vision that benefits the world, your creative province can become a community with magnificent possibilities.

5. CREATE THE PRIMARY VISION WITH A NAME OF DESTINY AND POWER

Names have destiny. We should always label ourselves (a label being a type of name), and never allow others to label us. This is one way we keep our own power. Likewise, people creating Provinces, like parents naming their child, must be very mindful of the name they are giving their creation.

The Primary Vision is so integral to the Province that it should be evident in the Province name. Such a province name will give power to the Province and its vision, and enable it to be easily identified.

If the area where the creative province is generally located already has "a Name of Destiny," use it to its full advantage.

> EXAMPLE: SWAN LAKES PROVINCE: A PROVINCE OF SWAN LAKE HABITATS, BALLET, AND GRACEFUL BEAUTY
>
> For example, a lake called Swan Lake might be a wonderfully appropriate place to start a Swan Lakes Province, for the reestablishment and protection of swans, for the lake probably was once home to many swans, and with a little help could once again be a suitable environment for them.
>
> But in this example the creators decide to go a step further: There are other lake communities in the region that wish to enhance their swan habitats; and there are also some ballet composers, dancers, and musicians who live in these lake regions. Thus, inspired by the lake's name, which is also the name of Tchaikovsky's famous ballet, the creators word their Vision as "A creative province of swan lake natural habitats, with one or more Ballet Theatres on the lakes' shores, and other swan-inspired artistic creations, such as swanlike boats and costumes."
>
> Thus the original lake's name empowers the Province, reviving its destiny as a central home for swans, and enhancing it with swan art and ballet.

Putting It All Together

The Creative Province Primary Vision, then, should be stated as an active, real place, with a succinct and positively stated goal that is of benefit to the world. And the Province should be given a Name of Destiny.

> *Example: The Monarch Butterfly Migration Corridor: A Province of Butterfly Habitats*

In this example, a Monarch Butterfly Migration Corridor might state its Primary Vision as: "A Province of Monarch Butterfly habitats along the butterfly's natural migration corridor." This is a powerful vision statement because it is a positive and succinct statement that focuses on what the creators want, and it benefits the world.

And the Province is further empowered by its name: The Monarch Butterfly Migration Corridor is a Name of Destiny because it describes the natural heritage of the Monarch—the living pathway that has existed for this gorgeous and important pollinator species since the dawn of Earth.

II. Create Supporting Visions to Further Shape Your Province

Merzouga, Morocco, Camels in Sahara Desert, iStock /IoanaCatalinaE

While Creative Provinces will have one Primary Vision, they will also add, either at the outset or over time, various Supporting Visions. These will be integral to the Primary Vision, further developing its main goal.

Thus the Supporting Visions will enhance and shape the Vision:

- How will you run the province?
- What kind of Environment do you want to create?
- What kind of Culture do you envision?
- What provincial Industries will help your Vision?
- And do you want to encourage certain types of travel, or travelways?

180 | *CREATIVE PROVINCES*

1. CREATE A VISIONARY SYSTEM TO RUN YOUR PROVINCE

Napoleon and his Staff, Ernest Meissonier, 1868

The basic Supporting Vision of any Creative Province must be the establishment of a Visionary System to run it. The Visionary System manages the Province's Vision, its Protective Visionary Rules, the mapping and chronicling of its Heritage Treasures, and helps manifest the real experiences that bring the province to life.

There are three important points to consider when creating your visionary system:

1. DESIGN YOUR VISIONARY SYSTEM TO BE SOMETHING WONDERFUL THAT FITS YOUR PROVINCE VISION

Probably the most important feature of your Visionary System is that you design it to be something wonderful that fits your Province Vision. Why make running your creative province drudgery, when you can make it fabulously fun?

For example, if you are creating Camelot, then create the Knights of the Round Table to run it!

2. INCLUDE VISIONARY-APPROPRIATE ACTIVITIES WITH THE RUNNING OF YOUR CREATIVE PROVINCE

Why run your creative province with boring meetings when you can run it with fun activities?

Putting these two principles together, here are some examples of running your creative province in an enjoyable way:

- If you are creating a Hot Air Balloon Province, form a Circle of Master Balloonists to run it, who meet at the start of a Province Flight.
- If you are creating a Cat and Mouse Province, create a fun and whimsical way to run it, such as a Circle of Advocats and Advomice.
- An Opera Province might devise a Music Committee to run itself, headed by a Choral Master; Lead Soprano, Alto, Tenor and Bass; Orchestra Conductor; and Master Composer, who sing the meetings in recitative.
- A Train of Thought Province might create a Steering Committee to run itself, headed by a Chief Engineer, Master Philosopher, Head Travel Guide, and Master Historian, who meet in the train dining car, over a gourmet meal, during special travels.
- A Rawhide Province might run itself with a Chief Cattleman, Provincial Sheriff, Chief Gunman, and Head Plains Ecologist, who meet around breakfast campfires.
- A Horse Road Province might run itself with a council that included a Master Equestrian, Carriage Master, and Road Master, who meet on horseback as part of Province Road Inspections.
- Renaissance Portugal might be run by a Chief Historian, Master Costumer, Battle General, Chief Travel Agent, Provincial Bishop, Chief Estate Agent, Royal Secretary, and so forth, who meet on holy days at a Castle Feast.
- An Organic Farm Province might create a Farm Council to run itself, which included a Master Gardener, Master Horticulturist, Master Husbandman, Dairy Master, and Fair Chief, who meet during regular Province Picnics.
- And a Province of Ancient Rome would certainly want to create a Senate and Caesar, modeled on the ancient empire, to run itself.

3. *Structure your Visionary System to have* OATS: *Oversight, Accountability, Transparency, and Simplicity*

All Province Visionary Systems are creative democracies. But no matter how whimsical and fun your Visionary System is, it must be structured to give the provincials the ability to oversee its operation, and to hold people accountable for their actions—in a suitably provincial way, of course.

You cannot have Oversight without both Transparency and Simplicity. Make your Visionary System both Simple and Transparent. For more on this, please review Principle 5: Creative Provinces Are Creative Democracies.

And what about Accountability? Make sure you create rules for what to do when there is a problem in your Visionary System. Make this accountability fit your Province Vision. If one of the Knights of the Camelot Round Table has done something unethical, devise a provincially suitable punishment for him, such as sending him off on a Crusade. See Section III, Create Rules to Protect Your Vision, for more on this.

> *Example: The North Pole's Toy Council*
> In this example, the Visionary System of a Province of the North Pole might be a Toy Council comprised of an elected Santa Claus and a delegation of Elves to run the Province. They might be chosen based on such things as toymaking abilities, management skills, and of course physical features: for Santa: white hair, a beard, and a considerable girth; and for the Elves: a diminutive stature.
>
> The Province might also have many outposts around the world, and decide to select its head Santa from numerous Representative Santas, such as is done by the College of Cardinals in selecting a Pope.
>
> The Province would need to have simple rules that allow for the provincials to easily monitor the Toy Council and hold them accountable for their actions. Was the election of Santa fair? Are the reindeer being treated humanely? Are all the good girls and boys receiving presents? If not, there should be rules in place that describe how Santa will step down, and the Elves select a replacement until a new vote can be conducted.

2. Envision Your Provincial Environment

Palm Trees Silhouettes on Guadalupe Beach at Sunset, iStock.com/RomoloTavani

When creating your Province, ask yourselves: What enchanting environments do we want to create? Be sure to think beyond visual landscape appearances, and include wildlife, and all the senses: sight, sound, smell, touch, and taste.

Consider your Provincial Heritage Treasures: Your Wildscape, Landscape, Airscape, Waterscape, Artscape, Soundscape, and Scentscape. What among these are appropriate for your Province to protect, enhance, revive, or create anew? Be especially cognizant of protecting the integrity of their states of being.

Provincial Landscapes

Creative Provinces large and small will want to define their landscape visions. Some examples:

- A Province of Faerie might have a landscape vision of fairy-lit mossy paths through forests and garden glens.
- A Sioux Nation Province might have a landscape vision of prairie with indigenous and heritage prairie plants and animals.
- A Three Little Pigs Province that has micro-farms with free-range pigs, might have a landscape vision of orchards, meadows, and wooded areas abounding with truffles.

Provincial Airscapes

Creative Provinces should identify, enhance, revive, and protect their Airscapes. This is important because our airscapes have been invaded by largely invisible chemical and electromagnetic pollutants, which creative provinces will want to mitigate and prevent. For example:

- A Birdsong Province might identify their airscape vision as having chemically clean and EMF-free air.
- A Land of Milk and Honey Province will certainly want to identify both clean air, free of bee-killing pesticides, and a microwave-free environment as their airscape vision, in order to protect their bee colonies.

Provincial Wildscapes

Most Creative Provinces will want to identify, enhance, revive, and protect their Wildscapes. For example:

- A Family Farm Province might identify landscape visions of hedgerows, wetlands, and woods for maintaining their wilderness base.
- A Living City Province might create wildscapes by enhancing their buildings with living roofs, to provide nesting grounds for birds.
- The wildscape vision of a Brer Rabbit Heritage Province might include not only many wildflowers, wild berries, and indigenous fruit trees, but also Brer Bear, Brer Fox, Jack Sparrow, Sister Crow, Riley Rabbit, Brer Possum, King Deer, Wiley Wolf, and of course, Brer Rabbit himself.

Provincial Waterscapes

If your creative province has a body of water, be sure to define your waterscape vision. This will help your Province to not only maintain the integrity of its water resources, but to enhance their beauty and usage as well. For example:

- A Willow Creek Province might have a waterscape that includes naturally clean creek water, row boat launches, swimming areas with small beaches and rope swings over

the water, fishing areas, creek-side picnic parks, water fowl nesting places, and benches and foot bridges.
- A Working Elephant Province might include in their waterscape a sizeable lake for elephant bathing.

PROVINCIAL SOUNDSCAPES

Most Creative Provinces will be well advised to establish Soundscapes. This is especially true in our technological age where it is easy to be invaded by mechanical noises of all types. Thus:

- A Rose Garden Province might create a Soundscape of birdsong and a certain degree of natural quietude.
- An Opera Province might establish a Soundscape with a tradition of spontaneously singing opera arias and recitative throughout the course of daily life.
- And a Sunset Vigil Province might have a Soundscape of the rhythmic waves lapping against the shoreline.

> EXAMPLE: THE SOUNDSCAPE OF AN ALPINE BELLS PROVINCE
>
> In this example, people in and around a mountain village create an Alpine Bells Province. The houses and several churches were built with beautiful heritage architecture, and the churches all have bells. The Province starts a tradition of having the church bells ring out in elaborate chimes for all sorts of occasions: to announce the hours of the day, as well as to announce births, deaths, and marriages; to announce important meetings; and to celebrate the many religious and secular holidays. They thus create a Language of Bells.
>
> The Alpine Bells Province soon attracts hand-bell choirs, chime choirs, bells on doors to announce visitors, and bells on bicycles. There are sheep in the valley, with the patriarch sheep being the bell wether. Prowling cats wear a tiny bell on their collars, and dogs have bells on their leashes.
>
> Some provincials also revive horse transportation, with bells on the carriages and sleighs. And certain provincials wear bells on their legs when engaged in the Province tradition of Morris dancing.

Provincial Scentscapes and Tastescapes

When creating your Province environment, be sure to consider what kind of Scentscape and Tastescape you want. For example:

- A creative province might have a certain scent that will be its signature: a perfume, a flower, or the aroma from a type of cuisine.
- Garden Provinces might want scentscapes of their flowers, and limit the competing and often overwhelming synthetic fragrances.
- Historic and Heritage Provinces will have fun reviving and showcasing the particular perfumes of their period.
- A Train of Thought Province might feature a particular perfume when visiting a particular city.

Provincial Artscapes

Many creative provinces will feature an Artscape: a type of art, such as modern sculpture; a particular artist, such as Van Gogh; a school of art, such as the Hudson River school; a type of design, such as mandalas; or a color pallet. For example:

- The Artscape of a Queen of Sheba Camel Caravan Trade Route might be its colorful, long and stately camel caravans gliding through its desert landscape, adorned with colorful silks worn by both camels and riders.
- The Artscape of a Province of the Angels might be its collection of angel statuary, murals, paintings, and ethereal provincial costume.
- The Artscape of a Velvet Rabbit Province might be its soft fabrics and rabbit motifs, to honor its population of wild rabbits.
- An Organic Cotton Province might have an Artscape of flags flying everywhere, replacing signs on buildings and streets. A new language of color and design on fabric will be displayed in gorgeous waves of flags flying along streets, through valleys, and over hills.

3. Envision Your Provincial Culture

Argentine Tango, iStock.com / Liniana Esperanza

What makes provincials so entirely different from people in the outside, global world, is their authentic cultures. Provincials create their own cultures, in which they engage in real activities and know each other as real people.

In contrast, living in a globalist, far-flung, two-dimensional world requires us to rely heavily on unknown people for our culture: to create roles for us, to give us our fashion, to teach us, to entertain us. This is not to say that some creative provinces won't want to adopt current "outside world" fashions and the like. Some will, such as non-culture-oriented provinces; but even these might eventually gain in their membership, certain people who will influence their culture.

When creating your Province, or when updating your Supporting Visions, ask yourselves: What do we envision as our Culture? What is to be our Style? What Roles do we want to create? What Activities do we want to become part of our culture? And what other Heritage Treasures are appropriate for our Province to revive or create anew?

Provincial Fashion

Personal adornment is the foundation creativity of the human being—it is the first step humans take to create the persona they desire. The fact that human beings are born naked is a sure sign that we are creative beings. Not only are we meant to design and wear an infinite variety of costumes and adornments as a way of expressing ourselves, but also it is necessary that we do so.

Unlike global fashion, which is time-linear (last year's fashions become worthless, and only what is new is valued), provincial fashion is a heritage treasure to be preserved and enhanced.

Whether it's a fashion that is being revived from a past culture, a new one that is being created, or some combination of the two, costume, hair design, and other adornments will be the personal expressions of the culture that provincials can display every day to validate their cultural vision.

A "provincial look" need not be elaborate. Something as basic as a school or work uniform can distinguish a creative province. Or a fashion feature could be something as simple as a type of flower, ribbon, item of jewelry, or hat. Provincial fashion can also be achieved by such things as defining who wears what and when. Thus:

- The choristers of a Choral Province might wear scarves of a certain design, scarves being the essential item for singers to wear to protect their throats from drafts, and the Choral Master might wear a specially designed scarf.
- A Highlander Sheep Herding and Wool Province might give their shepherds a provincially woven wool cloak and hat for their field rounds, and they might present their Chief Shepherd with an honorary shepherd's crook.
- And a Province of the Angels might encourage angelic fashions of all types, such as flowing, gossamer gowns and other ethereal-fabric costumes, as well as halos and golden breast plates.

Example: The Elaborate Costumes of a Louis XVI Province

In more culturally ambitious provinces, such as fantasy, and historic and heritage provinces—particularly those of the fashion-pinnacle ages of the Sixteenth through Nineteenth Centuries—provincials will want to enjoy including elaborate and gorgeous costumes and hair designs in their culture.

In this example, a Louis XVI Province revives the period's costumes of unparalleled beauty and extravagance. The men wear tricorn hats, powdered wigs, knee-length coats, knee britches, frilled linen shirts, silk stockings, and leather shoes with stacked heels.

The women display elaborate hair or wig designs, decorated with such ornaments as jeweled combs and ribbons. They wear mantuas, panniers, and gowns with open skirts and bodices displaying ruffled and lace petticoats and stomachers.

The Province has among its members, costume designers, hair and wig designers, and makeup artists who recreate the elaborate period fashions for their provincials. In addition, there are provincial artisans who restore or replicate such period accessories as jewelry, shoes, purses, and snuff boxes.

Provincial Body Features

"He had but one eye, and the popular prejudice runs in favor of two."
—Charles Dickens, *Nicholas Nickleby*

What the global non-culture sees as "weird" or a "physical defect" or an "ugly" trait, will be, in particular creative provinces, highly revered. For example, when people create provinces such as those based on fantasy tales, science fiction superheroes, or angelic and other-worldly beings, then people with those physical characteristics will be highly prized. Thus:

- Your large nose becomes a mark of great distinction and investigative prowess in a Detective Province.
- Fatness is the ultimate in pulchritude in a Rubenesque Province.
- Diminutive size is greatly treasured in the Province of Faerie, not to mention Oz and The North Pole.
- White hair might be a requirement for certain roles in a Province of the Angels.
- Blond hair (natural or from a bottle) will be a distinguishing trait in a God of Thunder Viking Province.
- All manner of oddities and differences might become membership requirements in a Different Folks Province.
- And Middle Earth might attract to it, all manner of hobbits, giants, dwarves, trolls, wizards, elves, and goblins, who don't have to do anything to adapt to their role except wear cos-

tumes—they are already very tall, very short and squat, very big and ugly, or very thin and boney—and they are greatly revered and loved for it!

> *Example: The Scars of Honor of an American Civil War Era Province*
> In some creative provinces, as in this example of an American Civil War Era Province, your scars will be your badge of honor. No matter where you actually lost it, when you are in a Historic War province, that missing limb represents a legacy from battle. You are not faking it—rather, you are honoring the many who lost limbs, their sight, and other faculties from the ravages of that war. You are honoring it by re-living it in this lifetime. In other words, in creative provinces, in addition to reenacting battles as a glorious activity, it may be just as important to honor and re-live the sacrifices that were made.

There is no end to the ways creative provinces might feature physical anomalies of various types. For example, what Pirate Province would be complete without its next-generation Captain Hook and his eye-patched and peg-legged mates? And the warrior archers of an Amazon Matriarch Province might be single breasted, even if the actual mastectomy was done for reasons of illness.

Then again, you might have *actually had* your arm torn off by a protective momma in a Bengal Tiger Province. And that slash across your face might have *actually happened* when you were out hunting in a Medieval Province with your falcon. And that limp you *really did* get when a steer mangled your leg in a Rawhide Province cattle drive, or a knight drove his lance through your thigh in a Camelot jousting tournament. Wow, what an exciting life you're having!

Provincial Roles

The greater world is limited in many ways, and one of those ways is in the limited number of roles people might assume. You could strive to be a real politician, nurse, scientist, factory worker, or carpenter, but the roles available for a real knight, shepherd, pharaoh, musketeer, swordsman, munchkin, gypsy, or pirate are very limited.

With creative provinces, however, new opportunities abound for Provincials to showcase their untapped abilities.

- A Province of Medieval Carcassonne might have an open range for shepherding and hunting, and so might elect a Master Huntsman and a Chief Shepherd.
- A Cheyenne Province might have roles for Chief, Medicine Woman, and members of a Tribal Council.
- In an Elizabethan Province, Shakespearean actors will certainly be gainfully employed.
- In a Sun Spirit Province, Mr. Sunshine might be selected at its annual Province's Summer Solstice Festival, where he presides over provincial activities throughout the year.
- A North Atlantic Independent Fishermen's Province would of course have its fishermen, restaurateurs, boat builders, hoteliers, and so on. But it also might create roles to provide leadership for its provincial industries: Lobster Master, Chief Aquatic Scientist, Master Seafood Chef, Chief Fishmonger, Chief Boatman, Net Master, First Concierge, and so on. And later, as the province's culture develops further, it might add roles such as Marine Artist Laureate, and Shanty Master.
- A Province of Classical Greece would want to create roles from its ancient heritage, which might include various levels of Oracle, Philosopher, Poet, and various Athletes for its revived Classic Olympiad. It would also have its Senators, Chorus, and *Douloi* (slaves) who, this time around, might be first-level students and apprentices who work their way up to higher roles.

Provincial Language

In today's world, dominant languages are developing, and where they aren't, we have computerized translations. It is certainly good that we can now fairly easily communicate with most people around the world.

However, we must also be vigilant in protecting our heritage languages and writing. If we don't revive and protect them, we will lose our history and heritage, for how else can we read the works of our ancestors and know how they acted and felt? We would have to rely on translators—but so much true and subtle meaning is lost in translation, and who knows how well they might translate, or if they have a particular bias that would skew their interpretation? And translations are also often not available, especially for the many obscure and extinct languages.

Cursive script, or longhand, is also disappearing and no longer being taught in many schools. How will those students be able to read their ancestors' letters?

Also disappearing are types of speech, such as addressing people formally, such as by their title and family name, as well as the traditional formal manners that often accompanied these, such as bowing and curtsying when meeting people.

When creating your province, consider whether you want to revive or preserve a language—especially important when reviving a heritage culture whose language has been largely lost. Also consider a patois, accent, or type of speech. And consider the behaviors and customs that accompany these speech patterns, and how they affect each other.

Secretive languages might also be employed. In an example of a proto-province, the Pumei, Nushu Cultural Village in China, has a school and a museum established to revive and preserve Nushu, a secretive women-only language that females used during the historic times of their oppression.

Consider also that, in the provincial world, language need not be a formal, complex thing. It can be a certain way of pronouncing a particular letter, using a lisp, or making a sound between certain words. The possibilities are endless.

- A Silly Province, which takes on silly behaviors as part of their culture (silly walks, silly games, and all manner of jokes, etc.), might decide to hone their Pig-Latin skills, as well as Gibberish, to be used at certain times, such as when visitors become too tiresome.
- A Farm Province might adopt a language custom of mimicking the sound of an animal when talking about it, or inserting "moo," "baah," etc., somewhere in their sentences.
- A Formal Province might adopt a tradition of clearing one's throat after hearing a cuss word.

II. CREATE SUPPORTING VISIONS TO FURTHER SHAPE YOUR PROVINCE | 193

PROVINCIAL BEHAVIORS, ATTITUDES, AND MANNERS

Behaviors, attitudes, and manners, as embodied in a cultural philosophy, are a form of Style. The beatniks of the 1950s, the musketeers of Renaissance France, and the monks, knights, and damsels of the medieval world, all had their own cultural philosophy, which produced behaviors, attitudes, and manners, which were as much a part of their style as were their physical appearances, languages, and roles.

In today's world, people are increasingly getting such behavioral, attitude, and manners guidance from the global media, which is controlled by unknown parties with unknown agendas. This is a slippery slope indeed. So, when creating your province, be sure to consider and define the behavioral aspects of the culture you want to create. Such behaviors, attitudes, and manners will be woven into the fabric of your province's customs. Be sure to adopt charming regular customs to enhance your provincial culture.

Here are some examples of regular customs a creative province might adopt:

- Customs for greeting fellow provincials, such as with shaking hands, bowing, or curtseying;
- Customs for calling on provincials, such as calling on them at home during their calling hours, and leaving calling cards;
- Customs for general communication, such as with hand-writing notes delivered by messenger;
- Customs for sending urgent messages, such as by displaying a certain flag at one's front door, or displaying a certain item of clothing on one's clothes line, or sending a note with a carrier pigeon;
- Customs for dining, such as eating at a low table while inclined on a chaise, in Ancient Rome; and
- Customs for entertaining, such as having cocktails while sitting in a hot tub in a Woodland Province.

In addition to such common daily customs, other customs will be major activities, such as barn-raisings or battle reenactments. These are discussed in Section V, "Activate Your Province with Real, Live Activities."

Example: The Manners of the Queen Victoria Province

In this example, a Queen Victoria Province has a strict code of manners that sets its standards of behavior.

Young people are chaperoned, and closely brought up by their parents with the help of other adult relatives and close friends of the family. Young Ladies "come out" at balls, where they are presented to society as being ready to receive gentlemen courtiers. The young men properly court young women ("dating" is a term unheard of here), and they, as well as other provincials, often communicate with the "language of flowers," giving flowers from one's garden to signify love, sympathy, contrition, good cheer, or even a warning of danger.

Men who offend a lady or a gentleman might well find themselves the recipient of a demand for satisfaction at one side of a dueling field.

Dress codes are strictly adhered to, such as for provincials in mourning, who wear mourning attire (black, and then progressively lighter shades of gray and purple) for a period of months. Letters are written by hand for every communication. Provincials have calling hours, and use calling cards.

Provincial Activities

Activities of all sorts, including holidays, general participatory events, work parties, warfare and athletic competitions, and rites of passage, are all critical elements of culture. These are described in the sixth step, "Activate Your Province with Real, Live Activities."

4. ENVISION YOUR PROVINCIAL INDUSTRIES

Portrait of forger studying handmade sword in workshop near furnace, Alfa27

All creative provinces, not just those classified as Industry Provinces, will have opportunities inherent in their visionary structure to develop provincial industries. For example, any creative province that has a provincial fashion vision will spawn small and micro industries of specialized costume designers, tailors, cobblers, jewelers, hair and wig designers, makeup designers, and shops for costume sales and rentals.

When you form your creative province, think about what industries will help you manifest your primary and supporting visions. For example, ask yourselves: What industries will help your provincials and guests easily participate in the activities you have in mind? What industries do you need in order to have a viable provincial transportation infrastructure? What industries will be essential in maintaining your environment, or history? These are the sorts of visionary industries you will want to encourage.

With creative provinces you have the opportunity to develop very specialized small and micro provincial industries, and to create internal marketing networks for them, in order to manifest your vision.

Externally, examples abound of small and micro industries that thrive in larger markets by specializing and by combining their efforts with other similar small and micro operations. Take for example the Amish who, with careful networking, successfully sell the products from their farms both within and outside their extended communities. In another example, independent authors and small book imprints successfully market their books through full-service print, marketing, and fulfillment companies that cater to them.

The following are some major categories of provincial industries to consider.

PROVINCIAL CULTURAL INDUSTRIES

Most creative provinces will develop a culture of some type, which will spawn industries such as:

- costume making and rental,
- instruction in provincial customs,
- language teaching,
- dance instruction,
- the teaching of provincial history, and
- provincial weapons industries.

PROVINCIAL KNOWLEDGE INDUSTRIES

Creative provinces can be places to go to, to work as an apprentice to learn a skill or a trade, or to immerse oneself in a culture to learn its language, art form, or history. Creative provinces might also be centered around universities, libraries, historical collections, and the like. Creative provinces might also be places where very specialized schools are established. Thus creative provinces will host a flowering of specialized educational industries.

Provincial Schools

The modern trend is toward large, all-inclusive schools and other mass-methods of educating children, which gravitate toward "a globally accepted truth." However, this "party line" is really not "the truth" at all: It is heavily influenced by all manner of competing interests to come up with one perspective of "the truth." They are also often now controlled by governments, and therefore must cater to a large heterogeneous group of students, with all manner of abilities and life goals. This practice of trying to shove each child into the same mold is a disservice to everyone involved.

Provincial schools, on the other hand, will be highly specialized, and will guard their own truths, resulting in the availability of many points of view, and the flowering of many types of abilities and life goals.

Provincial Universities

Creative Provinces might contain in their membership the departments of any number of universities that have study programs on their specific provincial subject.

For example, a Province of Ancient Egypt, whose Vision might be to restore the culture and science of Ancient Egypt, might include in its membership departments of Egyptology from universities around the world. The Province might then host these students in provincial lodgings to allow them to immerse themselves in the cultural life of Ancient Egypt.

Provincial Libraries and Bookstores

Similar to the situation with modern schools, the modern trend in libraries and bookstores is toward "large and all-inclusive." This is also true with online book sales, where *theoretically* you can find any book that ever existed. But this is a dangerous mindset to fall into. The reality is that the online world is becoming increasingly controlled by unknown parties—with books, films, and other documentation of alternative points of view in danger of disappearing down the Orwellian "memory hole."

Like a large department store, large libraries also contain a little bit of many things, but certainly not everything. The quality, depth, and uniqueness that come with specialization are missing. Large and complete selections on any particular topic are invariably missing. And often authors' independently published books are missing as well.

Also, the librarians at these large establishments have not read, and are often not even familiar with, most of their books. So to find a work on a specialized topic you usually have to research the topics online and search for the book online if you want any information in depth. But there we are again, back in the mysterious two-dimensional world of unknown controllers.

Specialized, provincial libraries and bookstores, on the other hand, will have the opposite approach. They might specialize in particular authors, genres, histories, or topics. Specialized libraries are the logical repositories and guardians of special collections, are depositories of in-depth knowledge, and are centers of research.

Provincial Visitation Industries

No matter what kind of creative province you have, it will become a specialized place that people will visit—to learn a certain thing, to get specialized products, or to experience life in a unique way.

Thus, creative province visitors will not be "tourists." They will participate in provincial activities, and might decide to look at real estate so that they can relocate to where the province is successfully manifesting. Thus they will need:

- travel agents,
- overnight accommodations,
- provincial transportation,
- visitor guides,
- concierges,
- language teachers,
- costumers,
- dance instructors,
- real estate agents, etc.

> *Example: Province Guides of an Edwardian Province*
> In this example, an Edwardian Province, as it grows, develops a provincial visitation industry. Such professionals as travel agents, concierges, real estate agents, costumers, and cultural guides join the Province.

A visitor might first be guided by a travel agent specializing in the Province. When the visitor arrives, he or she might then be attired with the help of a costumer; a cultural guide might teach them Edwardian manners; a concierge might involve them in provincial activities; and a dance instructor might teach them cotillion, country dance, scotch reel, and quadrille dances.

And if the visitor decides to join the Province, he or she might be guided by a real estate agent to properties located near important provincial hubs.

Provincial Environment Industries

Most creative provinces will have environments that will spawn environment industries. For example:

- Energy provinces will encourage such infrastructure industries as gas street lamps, solar panels, and wood stoves.
- Garden provinces will have their specialized garden centers, seed companies, garden equipment makers, fence builders, and gardeners and landscapers for hire.
- Featured Animal Provinces will want animal trainers, veterinarians, and equipment makers.
- Environmental restoration provinces will have environmentalists of varying types that will become expert in the projects the province undertakes, and be available for consultation and remediation work.

Provincial Transportation Industries

Envisioning provincial transportation and travelways is discussed in the next section. But think not only of the industries that create a transportation infrastructure, but also of the many correlating businesses that will be supportive of the vision lifestyle.

For example, Horse Provinces will want to encourage the provincial industries that create their infrastructure, such as horse breeders and trainers, stables, blacksmiths, farriers, carriage makers, saddle and harness makers, and carriage drivers.

Horse Provinces will also give rise to parking lots on their perimeters, cafés for waiting for one's carriage, and provincials will want riding attire that suit the visions of their province.

5. Envision Your Provincial Transportation and Travelways

Steampunk Airfield Vintage, ImaArtist/Pixabay

Creating a transportation infrastructure will be a major undertaking for many creative provinces, such as Historic and Heritage Culture provinces. Fortunately, it is the nature of creative provinces to grow organically and gradually, and so these undertakings need not be overwhelming, even if your vision is a large one.

Creative provinces with a transportation vision will also want to include in their Supporting Visions, plans to connect to both other creative provinces and strategic non-provincial places.

For example, if you are forming a Countryside Horse Province, and you envision your membership to be spread out all over a wide area, one of your Supporting Visions could be stated: "To connect Countryside Horse Province properties with a network of Horse Roads and trails."

> *Example: Establishing Period Horse Transportation in Old New York*
>
> In this example, people in various old neighborhoods in New York City create a Province of Old New York, and want to establish period horse transportation.
>
> They develop a gradual plan that includes identifying properties, such as parking garages and lots that could be

transformed into corrals and stables, and encouraging provincial horse transportation industries, such as hansom cabs and farriers.

Gradually the Province expands in both its area and its clout, and soon its horse transportation has a significant presence in its neighborhoods, in Central Park, and on streets connecting to provincial rail stations.

EXAMPLE: A RAINBOW BALLOON CORRIDOR CONNECTS TO OTHER CREATIVE PROVINCES

In this example, a Rainbow Balloon Corridor Province might have a Primary Vision of establishing a balloon corridor along air-current airways suitable to hot-air balloon travel. It might then also include in its Supporting Visions, "To connect to various other Creative Provinces along air-current airways, and to there establish balloon ports, to enlarge hot-air balloon travel capabilities, and to incorporate balloon travel in various creative province activities."

Along these air-routes might be such provincial outposts as The Land of Milk and Honey, an Oxen and Plow Province, a Queen of the Prairie Province, the Land of Oz, a Nature's Light Province, and a Sunset Vigil Province. The Rainbow Balloon Corridor Province thus might envision:

- establishing balloon transportation between these various creative provinces,
- gradually establishing balloon ports and amenities at their suitable field areas, and
- encouraging joint provincial activities at these various creative provinces, that include hot-air balloon travel.

III. Create Rules To Protect Your Vision

When Law Dulls the Edge of Chance, Charles M. Russell, 1915

Primary and Supporting Visions are the creative blueprints of a Creative Province. Province Rules are more specific, and are designed to protect the Vision.

Thus, if a Province's Primary Vision is akin to a Declaration of Independence, and Secondary Visions are like a Constitution, then the province's Rules are like the laws and regulations specifying how to interpret and follow the Constitution. Without such rules specifying how the Province Vision is to be followed, it would be open to very wide interpretation and the Vision could become corrupted.

One need only look to military services to see examples of how to protect a Vision. Military services are organizations where people live and follow certain visionary rules. And if you don't follow the rules, you are not promoted, are disciplined in an appropriately military way, or you are thrown out completely.

Sovereign Law vs. Provincial Rules

As described in Principle 7, creative provinces are not sovereign states; they are community organizations that will have rules to run themselves and manifest their visions. Thus provincials will abide by the laws of the sovereign state(s) in which they reside, and will participate in the sovereign states' services as appropriate, to the greatest extent under the Province Vision.

As an obvious example, historic and heritage provinces would follow today's universal laws against slavery, and adjust this historical aspect of their provincial cultures accordingly. Thus, the students and apprentices in Classical and Hellenistic Greece might be called slaves, or *Douloi*, but in name only, and would instead be treated like plebes.

> *Example: Pirates on the High Seas*
>
> In this example, a Seventeenth Century Province might allow under its visionary rules, provincial pirates of a Jolly Roger Province to periodically attempt to rob the Province's tall ships of their "treasure," using appropriate period weaponry. These provincial pirates may actually succeed in some of their plunder, but would not be prosecuted by the umbrella sovereign state governments; rather, swashbuckling provincials would seek them out to regain their stolen treasure.
>
> On the other hand, if someone outside of the province membership stole a Province's tall ship, or anything else, for that matter, then the sovereign state's justice system would step in with appropriate legal action.

The Seven Types of Province Rules

To establish your province rules, it will be helpful to categorize them under the seven types, described below.

1. Establish Rules for Running the Province

In creating a Province, it will first be necessary to establish rules on how to run the Visionary System: the frequency of meetings, the selection of officers, and so on. Remember to create the running of your province as a Vision-appropriate and fun activity.

> EXAMPLE: RULES FOR THE RUNNING OF CAMELOT

In this example, Camelot might establish, as its Visionary System, both a Knights and a Ladies of the Round Table. From there it would need rules on how these two parts of the full Round Table would be formed, and how it would run the Province.

Camelot might decide that the Knights and Ladies of the Round Table will consist of the King (Arthur II, etc.), the Queen (Guinevere II, etc.), and various Knights and Ladies chosen in its annual, midsummer "Camelot Pageant of Knights and Ladies."

The Province rules might further stipulate that the Round Table meet at each New Moon to make managerial decisions; and that at each season, on Lammas, All Souls, Candlemas, and Beltane, all provincials meet with the Round Table to make plans ...and celebrate!

> EXAMPLE: RULES FOR RUNNING A STAR TREK SPACE PORTAL PROVINCE

In this example, a Star Trek Space Portal Province might be established with a representative meritocracy visionary system, with an appropriately selected Board of Scientists to run the Province. From there it would need rules on how this Scientific Board would be formed, and how it would run the Province.

The Province might decide that its Scientific Board will consist of a group of eleven chief scientists, engineers, and architects, including an astrophysicist, an astronomer, a spacecraft engineer, and an architect. They might be chosen in an annual vote by all provincials in the Province's professional membership category, and meet weekly.

To make this an enjoyable activity, the Scientific Board might include in this annual meeting, a space trip to a nearby planet for all involved.

2. Establish Province Membership Rules

As stipulated in Principle Six, Creative Provinces are free and open within their protective visionary structure. In other words, like any other community organization, such as a church or community theater, anyone can join and participate if they follow the visionary rules.

For this reason, a creative province might want to have various kinds of memberships for people who wish to participate in different ways. For example:

- A creative province might have different membership categories for people living in different locations; for short-term and long-term members; for people with different types of skills, such as farmer, fisherman, toymaker, or shepherd; or for people who do certain work, such as help to maintain the horse road.

Some creative provinces will want to have contributory work requirements to manifest their Vision. For example:

- To manifest its Vision to restore its river, a Grandfather River Restoration Province might require that its member provincials work a certain number of hours each month in river ecological restoration work.

Some creative provinces will want to designate a particular physical appearance, condition, or ability for their provincials. For example:

- A Polar Bear Province might have a requirement that its members be able to run fast in order to escape bear attacks.
- A Warrior Province might stipulate that its provincials prove themselves in appropriate provincial battle contests.

Some creative provinces will want to designate a particular vocation as part of their Vision. For example:

- A Pacific Islands Fishermen's Province might have a requirement that its member provincials be independent fishermen, or be in an independent supporting occupation, such as fish marketer, seafood restaurateur, or boat builder, or contribute in some meaningful way to advancing the local fishing industry.

Many creative provinces will be fluid in terms of their location. Other creative provinces, though, will be very focused on a specific locality. For example:

- A Wilderness Province might have provincial outposts in many far-flung locations, with the goal of eventually connecting their land in wilderness corridors as more properties in-between are added.
- A Nile River Heritage Province might collect its membership from historic riverboat owners, and owners of property along its banks and watershed. However, someone who grew up on the river's shores but who now lives in Spain might join the province, and be a financial supporter. In such cases, different types of memberships could be created with a different set of participatory rules.

3. Establish Province Environment Rules

Many creative provinces will want to have rules for attaining a certain environment. Environment Provinces in particular, will necessarily require that their members meet their environment standards. For example:

- An Old Rose Heritage Garden Province might stipulate that provincials encourage Old Rose varieties in their Province gardens, and keep out rose hybrids.

If a creative province has a Soundscape Vision of any type, it will need to establish Province Rules on how that will be attained and maintained. It might have stipulations on such things as the decibel level of equipment, or the time, duration, and frequency of their use. For example:

- A Preservation Jazz Province Vision might be to preserve early-period jazz music. Even though it is not an Environment Province, it might establish Soundscape rules to prohibit electrified musical instruments, amplifiers and other electronic sound systems and music styles outside of the early Jazz Age.

4. Establish Province Cultural Rules

No matter how ambitious a creative province's culture, it will want rules to protect that culture. For example:

- A Sunrise Bicycle Province might have rules on strict manners on how to behave politely on its bicycle roads.
- A Meditation Province might have strict rules against jibber-jabbering.
- An Oak Hills Artisan Furniture Province might have rules against bad-mouthing any fellow Province artisans, except by complaint through accepted Province channels.

> *Example: The Queen Victoria Province's Book of Manners*
>
> In this example, a Queen Victoria Province might have as its Primary Vision: "A Province of Victorian Period Lifestyle." Its supporting visions might include statements embracing Victorian-era travel, period farming techniques, open ranges for sheep herding, and Victorian architecture, costume, dance, and manners.
>
> To guide provincials and visitors on how to interpret these visions, it might adopt several rule books, such as a Book of Victorian Manners, which describes the customs and behavior of the Period—guiding everything in day-to-day life, including the proper running of a household, entertaining, appropriate attire, correspondence, courtship, marriage, birth, death and funerals, forms of address, dance step instructions, and the meanings of presented flowers.

5. Establish Province Visitation Rules

Creative provinces don't have "tourists;" they have "participating visitors."

Students of a certain subject can thus immerse themselves in provincial life, and live its culture, such as speaking the provincial language and learning its history and heritage. And creative provinces will want to have rules regarding such participation.

Example: Visitor Requirements for Camelot

For example, in Camelot, you might apply to visit, and once accepted, you would don the Camelot fashion, manners, language, and other accouterments, and experience Camelot as (depending on your qualifications) a knight, damsel, squire, scullery maid, monk, gardener, or some other role.

And who would be denied entry? Camelot would certainly want to deny entry to visitors not in period attire or who refused to leave behind electronic equipment. And if you dared to debase the Camelot culture with modern profanity, you would certainly be thrown over the parapet by some guardian knight.

Example: Guest Requirements for a Wyatt Erp Province

A Wyatt Erp Province might require that its guests not gain entry unless attired in Western garb, are not carrying modern devices, and have a mode of transport that is either pedestrian, by train, by hot-air balloon, or horse-based.

And if a tender-footed fool tried breaking one of this Province's rules, he might end up on the wrong side of a gunfight.

Example: Modes of Travel Through a Carcassonne Medieval Province

As a creative province grows and develops political clout, it will be able to affect rules governing how its roads are used.

For example, if the province's borders have become secure, such as in the case of gated communities, then access to its roads can be controlled so as to maintain their integrity and purpose. With the obvious exception of government and emergency representatives, people could be denied entry if they did not comply with province rules.

In this example, a Carcassonne Medieval Province, as its membership grows and develops political clout, and its properties cover contiguous streets, would eventually be able to work through the appropriate government channels to close those streets to automobile traffic, allowing only pedestrians, equestrians, and similar period travel.

III. CREATE RULES TO PROTECT YOUR VISION | 209

6. RULES FOR HANDLING DEVIANTS

And how would you deal with the provincials and visitors who break the province's rules? If the breach is serious, the province membership might be revoked, or a visitor might be banned for all eternity.

But province traditions might also be established where a punishment that is "appropriate to the Vision" is done to those who didn't comply with the province's rules.

EXAMPLE: COLONIAL AND REVOLUTIONARY AMERICA PROVINCE'S HANDLING OF DEVIANTS

> A Colonial and Revolutionary America Province might adopt several rules for handling deviants:
>
> First, how to deal with the scoundrel who refuses to wear the tri-corn hat? It is decided that, assuming the man can swim, he is to be thrown into a handy pond by the burliest male provincials available.
>
> Second: How to deal with captured British spies! It might be decided that male spies are to be "shot" by a firing squad—which actually could entail stripping him naked, tying his hands behind his back, and "borrowing" one of those futuristic devices with a "lightning flash" to capture his image on paper, which would then be posted in the Province square with the heading "Redcoat Spy!"
>
> A supporting vision could be established that the Province will hold frequent and regular fencing matches, which would have the added benefit of training its young men for future martial encounters with the Redcoats. Then a rule could be made from this, whereby a provincial could demand satisfaction via a fencing duel when a fellow provincial or visitor behaved badly.

7. SAFETY RULES

Will creative provinces have dangers? For example, might you be eaten by a big cat in a Bengal Tiger Province? Or plummet to your death in the Rainbow Balloon Province and Balloon Corridor?

Well, of course! Such dangers "come with the territory," just like living in today's "global automobile province" subjects one to automobile accidents. All activities have their unique dangers.

Thus, to minimize the dangers inherent in motorized vehicle travel, today's "global automobile province" society has established many safety rules: for pedestrians, for car manufacturing, and for operating the vehicles.

Similarly, creative provinces will need to establish their own safety protocols suited to their special environments.

> *Example: A Countryside Horse Road's Rules*
>
> All animal-centered provinces will want to establish rules for the humane treatment of their animals, and for the safety of the animals and people, unless the laws of the surrounding sovereign government are sufficient to meet the needs of the province.
>
> In this example, a Countryside Horse Road might have rules for pedestrian and equestrian safety, including signs such as those indicating who has the right of way on its bridal paths. It also might have established rules for the humane treatment of horses that go beyond the laws of the surrounding sovereign government.

> *Example: A Bengal Tiger Province's Rules*
>
> A Bengal Tiger Province would probably want to establish basic safety rules for avoiding tiger attacks. For example, the Province might have certain areas or time periods that are off-limits to lone hikers; it might require certain safety classes for provincials and visitors; and it might require that certain equipment be used for protection.

IV. Accumulate and Chronicle Your Heritage Treasures

Carcassonne and Vineyard, iStock.com/namibelephant

It is critical that a creative province chronicle its Heritage Treasures from the start so that they may be claimed as part of the province, and be maintained, protected, restored as need be, and used to manifest the Province Vision. The Heritage Treasures Chronicle should include both a written account and a map.

The Province Chronicle should be maintained throughout the life of the creative province.

The nature of creative provinces is that they will grow or shrink when provincials add or delete their correlated property. Thus creative provinces should design both the written account and the map so that they can be updated simply, and can become as elaborate and complex as necessary.

The creative province should chronicle all six types of Heritage Treasures, as stated in Principle Four: The Province's 1) Membership, 2) Correlated Real Property, 3) Correlated Natural Resources, 4) Correlated Personal Property, 5) Correlated Industries, and 6) Correlated Information, History and Culture. The chronicle should include descriptions of the Heritage Treasures, including their condition.

We will describe the actions needed to accumulate and chronicle your heritage treasures under three headings: 1) Add and connect provincials and property; 2) Map and connect your heritage treasures; and 3) Chronicle your province heritage treasures.

1. Add and Connect Provincials and Property

Once you have started your creative province, it is time to add provincials and their correlated property.

Adding Individual Provincials and Groups

The basic way a creative province grows is by individuals and groups who have the same Vision, becoming members.

These member provincials also bring with them their correlated properties, skills, and other heritage treasures. In this way a creative province gradually grows and organically takes shape as it collects, under its umbrella, the correlated properties of its provincials.

For this reason, it is the Provincials who are the creative province's basic Heritage Treasure through which all other heritage treasures exist.

A creative province may add to its membership not only individuals, but also certain organizations and other groups, such as historical societies, eco-villages, or government-owned parks. For example:

- A Colonial and Revolutionary America Province might have as its Vision, the preservation of the heritage of the period surrounding Colonial America and the American Revolution. It would then bring into its membership both individuals and

groups, such as historical societies, museums, battlefield park organizations, battle reenactment groups, sewing groups, and chapters of the National Society of the Sons of the American Revolution and the Daughters of the American Revolution.
- A private panther corridor organization might form a Panther Migration Corridor Province to expand its reach, adding to its provincial membership residential property owners, ranchers, ecologists, environmental groups, and government agencies of many different sovereign states in the panther's traditional territory.

Example: Adding Provincials to a Province of The North Pole

In this example, various toymakers form The North Pole, an Industry Province with the Vision of a bringing to life the Santa myth, making toys, decorations, and other gifts for distribution at Christmas, Yule, Hanukah, Kwanzaa, and other celebrations of the winter season. Provincials all have some role in the industry, such as the making and distribution of toys and decorations.

Because there are people the world over who want to join this Province, it sets up a sophisticated computerized method for keeping track of its provincials and their roles. Eventually there are thousands of Santa Clauses, Kitty Clawses, shopkeepers, and many artisans who make toys, ornaments, costumes, and so on. A vast system of information and distribution develops, with provincials sharing their wares, and making sure that all good girls and boys, and kitties and doggies too, get toys.

Included among The North Pole's membership are not only individual artisans and distributors, but also such organizations as toy companies and already-existing distribution networks that wish to be a part of the Province's Vision and its vast network.

Combining Creative Provinces and Connecting Them with Province Travelways

As they grow, creative provinces with much in common will discover each other and might decide to merge. When two or more such provinces combine, their Primary and Supporting Visions might need to be restated to reflect the new combined primary and supporting visions.

These creative provinces might also want to form Province Travelways between them, to facilitate their connection.

> *Example: Combining and Connecting Horse Road Provinces*
>
> Several unconnected Horse Road Provinces might form in a particular region, and then combine in order to extend their Horse Roads and facilitate their eventual connections.
>
> In this example, a Countryside Horse Road becomes an extensive network of horse roads and trails throughout a rural region. In a nearby area, an Old Farm Horse Road exists as a provincial travelway that extends through a region of old-style farms.
>
> The two province travelways then decide to combine and rename themselves the "Old Farm Countryside Horse Road." They thus extend their reach and grow in membership and clout.

Connecting Creative Provinces Using Province Federations

Creative provinces with similar or Complementary Visions can join together to form Province Federations, for the purpose of mutual benefit. As with the provinces themselves, creative province federations can overlap, and exist inside one another. Creative provinces can also belong to many province federations, and remove themselves from such federations if they so choose.

> *Example: A Federation of British Heritage Monarchy Provinces*
>
> In this example, a group of British Heritage Monarchy Provinces, which includes a Victorian Province, a Tudor Province, a Georgian Province, and a Medieval England Province, forms a Federation of British Heritage Monarchy Provinces. The federation decides to be under the umbrella provincial rulership of the current British monarch, with each of the various heritage provinces under the sub-rulership of their particular heritage royal family. Thus the federation has its current-time Queen or King, while at the same time, Elizabeth I, Queen Victoria, various King Henrys, King Arthur, and others reign in their respective heritage provinces.

In other words, with creative provinces we can reach across time with different eras coexisting and interacting.

Thus, the Renaissance Province of Elizabeth I might hold a glorious fete: a pageant that includes a combined-history tournament, to which are invited all the other historic provinces of the federation, as well as the current royal personages, to participate.

EXAMPLE: FAIRY TALE PROVINCE FEDERATION

In this example, a Fairy Tale Province Federation is formed to connect numerous Fairy Tale Provinces from around the globe.

Among the member creative provinces are those that bring alive the fables of Aesop, the famous slave and storyteller of ancient Greece; the fairy tales and nursery rhymes of the German brothers Jacob and Wilhelm Grimm; the fairy tales of Sweden's Hans Christian Anderson; and the Uncle Remus stories of Brer Rabbit and his friends of the early African-American South.

These creative provinces connect as a federation for mutual support, such as in making their provincial whimsical realities more accessible to visitors.

EXAMPLE: A FEDERATION OF ORGANIC PROVINCES

In this example, a Federation of Organic Provinces includes thousands of Organic Farm Provinces, Organic Garden Provinces, and Organic Cottage Industry Provinces. These member provinces may themselves overlap in numerous locations.

Certain of these member provinces might also belong to other federations: For example, an India Organic Cotton Province might belong to both a Federation of Organic Provinces and a Federation of India Heritage Provinces.

One of the main purposes of the Federation of Organic Provinces is to help its member provinces share many resources, such as information, legal assistance, and marketing networks.

EXAMPLE: A FEDERATION OF RIVER AND STREAM RESTORATION PROVINCES

In another example, a Federation of River and Stream Restoration Provinces might include hundreds of River and

Stream Restoration Provinces from around the globe. The Federation might provide to its member provinces, expert advice and political support for such activities as the removal of obsolete dams, pollution abatement, and the revival of waterways travel.

Example: A Federation of Warrior Provinces

In this example, various creative provinces might form a Federation of Warrior Provinces, for the purpose of, among other things, coordinating war games and related activities between their member provinces.

The Federation's member provinces might create such activities as new battles between different types of warriors (for example, Roman Legions against Medieval Knights); battle revision enactments between Heritage Provinces, where the outcomes might be different from the historic battles; and festive tournaments where the warriors display their abilities with weapons of their period, such as sword, lance, long bow, and six-shooter.

Example: Camelot Joins Several Federations

In another example, Camelot might initially join a Federation of Medieval Provinces, and then later decide to also join a Federation of Old Europe and Fantasy Provinces. And even later, those two federations may decide to expand beyond Europe and become members of a worldwide Federation of Old World and Fantasy Provinces.

2. Map and Connect Your Heritage Treasures

An individual or group starting a creative province begins with mapping their property as the first property. It doesn't matter if the property is a vast tract of land, or something as simple as a rented flat. The point is that you are saying to the world that *you* are beginning a creative province *here*.

The Creative Province Map has many purposes, both for visionary planning, and for daily maintenance:

- It shows where the creative province is currently located and taking shape.
- It lets prospective provincials know where province hubs are developing so that they can be guided on where they might want to buy or rent property.
- It can show where key connecting properties exist.
- It can show the locations of nearby properties for sale.
- It can show the properties of people who might want to join the province.
- A map of a province road will show where ideal connecting properties lie, and where alternative routes exist.
- A province road map that is kept current can also show where there are roadblocks and detours.
- It can show where wildlife is migrating, or where cattle are being herded or driven.

Various Ways to Map a Creative Province

There are many ways to map a creative province—from sophisticated computerized maps, to hand-drawn maps of the kind our ancestors drew. Thus:

- A map of a Peter Pan Province for Young Families that is mainly located in an apartment building might look like floor plans;
- A Sun-Spirit Province might use a County Property Map to show which properties belong;
- A Renaissance Province might use hand-drawn maps that are displayed in various provincial enclaves; and
- The map of an African Elephant Migration Corridor might use a computer-mapping program that can zoom out to cover the African continent, and zoom in for close-up views of the Province properties that comprise the corridor. It could also show the locations of the current migrations.

Whatever kind of Province Map is used, it should be kept current; made available to the provincials so that they will know the parameters of their Province territory; and made available to people searching to join the province and perhaps obtain property near a provincial hub.

Example: Mapping an Old West Province Road

In this example, an Old West Province Road might use an Internet mapping program to keep its travelways current. It would include the current status of hot-air balloon airways, stagecoach runs, wagon trains, rail lines, horse trails, and cattle drive routes. Provincial properties would be included on the map, with a zoom feature, and another feature would allow for notations of specific information, such as temporary detours or cautions.

Example: Mapping the Apartment Properties of a Songs of Sunlight Canary Province

In this example, a Songs of Sunlight Canary Province might begin in a garden apartment complex, to house a colony of canaries. The Province would want their map to show the various floors of the buildings, as well as the common aviaries that have been built to abut these apartments.

Later, if the Province connects with similar canary provinces at a distance, it might have several such maps.

Mapping Provinces That Overlap

Creative provinces can overlap, and there can be provinces within provinces. For example:

- A large and extensive Horse Province might overlap, or have within it entirely, garden provinces, historic and heritage provinces, quiet provinces, and wilderness restoration provinces.
- Creative Provinces in the Western US might overlap: a Zane Gray Province; a Buffalo Open Range Province; a Red River Restoration Province; a Plains Indian Province; an Old West Province Road; a Cowboy Open Range Cattle Province; and a Sunshine Solar Energy Province.

3. Chronicle Your Province Heritage Treasures

It is essential that creative provinces chronicle their many Heritage Treasures so that they may be properly maintained, protected, appreciated, properly used, and revived or restored if they have been lost or depleted.

To chronicle their treasures, creative provinces might use any number of means, including handwritten logs, computer spreadsheets, and sound and visual recordings, as well as good old-fashion memory in the form of language, stories, and songs.

Province Membership, and Correlated Skills, Personal Property, and Industry Treasures

Creative provinces will need to chronicle their member provincials, with descriptions that include their correlating provincial features, personal properties, skills, and industries.

> *Example: Chronicling the Provincials of The North Pole*
>
> A North Pole Province might include in its log of member provincials: its Primary Santa and Mrs. Claus; its Primary Elves; and its many Second-, Third-, and Fourth-Level Santas and Elves around the world; and its many other provincials who are in supporting roles, such as toy makers, toy shop owners, and toy distributors, as well as reindeer ranchers and sleigh-makers.
>
> The log would include pertinent correlating information about the provincials, such as their particular skills in toy making; their toy distribution networks; and their correlating physical characteristics in the case of the Santas and Elves.
>
> The Province of The North Pole would also want to chronicle certain of its provincials' personal properties that correlate with the Province Vision. For example, some members might own reindeer, sleighs, and costumes, which they might make available to others in the Province in various circumstances.

Province Real Property and Natural Resource Treasures

Creative provinces will need to chronicle their member provincials' land, architecture, infrastructure, and other real property, if these correlate with the Province Vision. They will also need to chronicle their correlated Natural Resource Treasures, including the integrity of such.

Land: The correlated land properties of the member provincials should be documented and included in the Province's list of treasures. These would be properties such as the tiny houses of a Tiny House Province; the rose gardens of a Heritage Rose Province; the provincial properties along the stream of a Stream Restoration Province; the ranges and herding trails of a Rawhide Open Range Province; and the castles of a Medieval Province.

Other Property: Other important property belonging to the provincials that correlates with the Province Vision should also be chronicled. These might be such things as the musical instruments of a Preservation Jazz Province; the period wardrobes of a Medieval Province; the environmental equipment of a Dark Skies Province; and the horses and equestrian equipment of a Countryside Horse Province.

The level of detail in such chronicles will depend on how assiduous the creative province wanted to get. For example, a heritage province might want to mention which provincials have adequate period wardrobes, but not get into the detail of how many items of clothing; whereas it might want to record the model, make and condition of its fleet of vintage automobiles.

Wilderness and Natural State of Being Treasures: Be sure to chronicle all your creative province's wild areas and wildlife, and their condition. Natural-state-of-being treasures include the integrity of the air, water, and soil; the natural quietude and dark skies; and so forth.

> *EXAMPLE: CHRONICLING THE CORRELATED TREASURES OF A GOD'S FIELDS PROVINCE*
>
> In this example, provincials of a God's Fields Province have obtained farmland from a defunct corporate farm where the soil has been greatly damaged from years of GMOs, chemical pesticides, and other harmful practices.
>
> The Province will need to chronicle its farmland properties, as well as the condition of the soil at various locations;

the wildlife, or absence thereof; the water quality of streams; and so on.

As the Province develops and restores farmland, it will need to update the chronicle to record its successes with such endeavors as land restoration and viability.

Province Information, Historic, and Cultural Treasures

There have always been various amounts of censorship throughout history. Therefore it is imperative that creative provinces protect their information. Original prints of books, films, and other documentation need to be physically preserved in provincial libraries; languages need to be preserved through their regular use; and histories can be further protected in song, visual arts, and storytelling.

Example: A Sitchin Antediluvian Library

In this example, a Sitchin Antediluvian Province might include in its primary Vision, the creation of an Antediluvian Library, which would include of the translation works of Zechariah Sitchin, as well as his source materials.

The Province might also seek to obtain other antediluvian texts for its Library, such as were originally in the great Library of Ancient Alexandria. That library contained no less than the accumulated knowledge of Humanity's origins and the engineering knowledge of the builders of the pyramids and other mathematically advanced structures based on the measurements of the solar system.

To ensure the safety of its historic and heritage information, the Province might place its information collection in numerous places, and take other security measures, since libraries can be destroyed by any number of means.

V. ACTIVATE YOUR PROVINCE WITH REAL, LIVE ACTIVITIES

Battle of the Sea, © 2002 by Marjory Harris

And finally we come to the truly fun and exhilarating part of provincial life: its real, live activities.

First, it is essential that your creative province establish real activities that support your Province Vision. These activities might span the range from simple to elaborate.

Many of these activities will become province traditions and thus heritage treasures. They will include such things as provincial holidays and holiday activities, rites of passage, festivals, special meals, work parties, games, artistic showings, demonstrations, debates, provincial court hearings, dances, athletic competitions, war games, and duels. The list of possible real, live activities is endless. We will describe some of them under four general categories: Holiday and General Participatory Events and Gatherings; Work Parties; Provincial Warfare, Dueling, and Athletic Competitions; and Provincial Rites of Passage.

Holiday and General Participatory Events and Gatherings

Here we have the all the participatory activities not covered in the next three categories of work parties, warfare/athletic events, and rites of passage. Of course there will be many holiday festivals that are widely practiced today, that will take on a provincial hue, such as a Medieval Christmas or a Victorian St. Valentine's Day. In addition to those, the following are just a few examples to illustrate the great scope of other holiday and participatory events and gatherings that creative provinces might engage in:

- A Sun-Spirit Province might hold monthly Mother/Father Sun Spirit religious ceremonies, as well as annual solar gatherings with sunflower competitions and seed exchanges.
- A Choral Province might hold periodic choral gatherings where they perform new compositions and hold choral competitions.
- A Space City might host regular astronomical space-travel tours.
- An Angel Province might hold soul-connection workshops.
- A Patty Cake Province might host Baking Fairs, displaying everything from angel food cakes to pizzas, with highly coveted baking prizes.
- A Countryside Horse Road Province might have a tradition of Trail Luncheons, where provincials ride or drive their carriages along their trails to a clearing, where a delicious field luncheon awaits them, which provincials take turns preparing.
- The men of a Tombstone Cowboy Province might bring back the tradition of sleeping out under the stars, where they tell their ancestor's Gold Rush stories and sing "Ghost Riders in the Sky."
- And any creative province might adopt such activities as performing plays, holding readings, hosting soirees, playing lawn games, or recording heritage stories on film. The possibilities are endless.

> *Example: Jane Austen Province Grand Balls and Socials*
> In this example, a Jane Austen Province establishes regular grand balls, where provincials, dressed in period costume, dance Regency dances such as *La Boulangere,* mentioned in Austen's works, accompanied by a provincial orchestra.

The Province also has regular Dance Socials, where provincials practice the Quadrille and Cotillions with provincial string quartets. And it also has regular Costume Socials, where provincials gather to design and sew their period costumes. Of course, gossip flies, and scrumptious teas are served.

Provincial Work Parties

Recall the words of Mark Twain cited earlier: *Work and play are words used to describe the same thing under different conditions.* This is important to remember when creating provincial "work parties." You are having fun accomplishing something with others. You get both the satisfaction of accomplishing something, as well as the opportunity to engage in a social event.

And so here we have activities that accomplish provincial work, but which become wonderful events because people are doing them together as a social activity. The following are just a few examples to illustrate the great scope of such work parties that creative provinces might engage in:

- An Organic Farm Province might revive the tradition of barn-raisings, combined with elaborate picnics. It might also hold various harvesting parties, such as Berry Picking, Cotton Picking, and Haymaking, followed by Barn Dances.
- A ColorSails Lake Province might have a tradition of Boat Painting Parties, where provincials gather to paint their boats bright colors, followed by lantern-lit outdoor dances along the shore.
- A Dog Province might hold regular Dog Training Saturdays, where provincials bring their dogs for training activities—tracking being the favorite—followed by dog playtime while provincials socialize with pizza and beer, and of course dog biscuits, all baked items made on their dog-shaped outdoor brick oven.

Provincial Warfare, Dueling, and Athletic Competitions

Over the course of its evolution, Humanity has striven to observe in many societies, laws of war (both written and unwritten) to dictate how adversarial contests would be fought. In particular, warrior classes were to follow religious laws to leave civilians and the wounded alone, and such types of honor among fighting men were paramount. Many societies had warrior classes that honed their fighting prowess to perfection, and for whom death in battle was the most honorable way to die.

Certain battles were great creations, and their art has been captured on canvass and in film, and have been reenacted by many historical societies.

Individual contests, such as dueling, when following certain strict rules, were also considered honorable means for men to resolve conflicts.

Thus in recreating heritage societies, as well as in creating new societies, creative provinces can take the best from the rules of our ancestors to conduct martial contests, and revive these contests in an artistic fashion.

So let's define provincial warfare and dueling:

> *Provincial warfare and dueling are mutually agreed-upon martial contests between provincial adversaries, exclusively using mutually agreed-upon provincial combatants, provincial weapons, and other provincial parameters, such as provincial uniforms for the identification of combatants.*

A creative province might choose to have traditional warriors who fight individually in duels, or in groups in battles. In such provinces, the provincials might choose their weapons and their numbers, and the fighting would be done under these controlled circumstances. For example, I envision that many years from the publication of this book, that such things as great fleets of tall ships will be back on Earth's oceans, and that their provincial owners will engage periodically in monumental maritime war games—provincial Olympic-type events of great planning.

Provincial athletic competitions will also be very specialized. Old games will be revived, and new games created. Provincials will be physically at their games, and participating in some way, including as the cheering audience.

Much fun can be had within and between creative provinces. For example:

- A Motorcycle Province might have an arrangement with a Quiet Province to "invade" them once a year and have a loud party.
- A Space Age Province might conduct a battle with a Cowboy Province.
- A Renaissance Province will certainly want to hold periodic sword fights.

Example: The Vikings Invade Ancient Rome

In this example, a God of Thunder Province, a Viking Heritage Province, might periodically engage in provincial attacks on other creative provinces, such as Celtic Ireland. In this example, it might be that it has grown enough in size and strength to allow it to be more ambitious—enough to invade Ancient Rome. Roman soldiers immediately prepare for attack and use their time tested warrior methods to combat the Northern Menace.

Example: Dueling in a Georgian Province

In this example, a Georgian Province revives its charming heritage tradition of dueling to address insults, redress grievances, or to get rid of competing suitors. The Province has several different types of martial contests suited to the nature of the situation, such as fencing; public debates with the loser buying everyone a round of drinks; and, of course, dueling pistols.

Provincial Rites of Passage

Creative provinces have the opportunity to create enchanting rites of passage traditions. For example:

- In a Bird Sanctuary Province, newborns might be brought outside for their first dawn chorus of bird song.
- In a Water Province, mothers might give birth in a designated lagoon, with mermaid midwives assisting.
- In a Renaissance Province, a young man's coming of age might be marked by a test of swordsmanship.
- In a Matriarchal Amazon Province, a young woman has to demonstrate archery skills, as well as recite her matrilineage going back five hundred years.

> *EXAMPLE: A TEUTONIC PROVINCE'S MUSIC TRADITIONS*
> In this example, a Teutonic Province features the works of Wagner, and has a tradition of its provincial orchestras and choruses performing at all important events: the "Bridal Chorus" from *Lohengrin* sung at Province weddings; "Wach auf" from *Die Meistersinger* sung for the occasion of the birth of children; and guests to the Province welcomed in a great hall with the "Arrival of the Guests at Wartburg" from *Tannhäuser*.
>
> At funeral rites, provincial choristers sing the "Pilgrim's Chorus" from *Tannhäuser*. And very renowned personages are honored with the choral salute from *Das Rhinegold*, "Entrance of the Gods into Valhalla."

> *EXAMPLE: A STARLIGHT PROVINCE'S BIRTH CUSTOMS*
> In this example, a Starlight Province, a dark-sky province of stargazers, astrologers, and astronomers, forms a custom whereby newborns are taken outdoors and passed in the arms of provincials dancing and humming to soft drumming, under the starlight. There the child is given its Star Name.

> *EXAMPLE: CREATIVE PROVINCE DEATH AND FUNERARY CUSTOMS*
> If you are truly ready to leave this earthly life, then death is a wonderful thing. And as with other customs, we can make our Death Rite of Passage an incredibly beautiful and meaningful send-off:

- A Great Sunrise Bicycle Road Province may have a tradition that when a provincial is ready to die, they go on a Last Ride with their fellow provincials.

- A Province of Ancient Rome might conduct funeral rites for special personages, such as the Caesar or senators, using funeral pyres instead of mortuary crematories.
- It used to be that the greatest honor for a warrior was to die in battle, and he would be forever rewarded in Valhalla or some other warrior heaven. Provincial battle traditions might include a significant way for a dying person to honor those who sacrificed their lives in a historic event.
- A Sacred Grove Province might have huts in their beautiful orchards for people wishing to fast and meditate when they are ready to pass on.

Adam Receives Divine Creative Inspiration, by Vance A. Larson

Conclusion

We now have, and indeed have always had, a great opportunity to live the lives Humanity was meant to live. We can create unlimited communities to help us live the lives of our fondest dreams. We can take inspirations from our favorite writers, artists, and filmmakers; from utopians and historians; from the experiences and wisdom of our ancestors and from the fresh ideas of our progeny.

We do not have to live in a world that someone else is imagining and is forcing upon us "from the top down." For example: We do not have to go along with a globalist corporate vision of an insensate technocratic superstate run by a tiny "elite" group that controls the rest of the world with computer chips.

What makes us provincials so entirely different from people in that construct is our unmatched authenticity. We are not gene-altered, artificially intelligent trans-humans. We create our *own* reality; purveyors of propaganda do not create it for us. While we use tools of all kinds, including some that are two-dimensional, we engage in real-life three-dimensional activities, interacting with and knowing each other as real people.

With Creative Provinces we manifest a magnificent Vision: *a vast, decentralized, living empire*, one that is formed with love, freedom, and consciousness "from the roots up."

We are *the Creative Empire*, where the Divine Creator rules, through His creative spirit, which resides in each of us. We humans are, after all, made in His image. We are *meant* to create.

And now we can especially create, with others, magnificent communities. We can grow "from the roots up" to create infinite places of wonder, beauty, and enchantment. We can create communities with real-life fun and opportunities to be unique and authentic. We can engage in meaningful work that we are eager to do and which gives us great satisfaction. We can commune with animals and all creatures in humane ways that allow them to thrive in all manner of goodness and love. We can create the most enchanting environments, activities, and travelways imaginable.

And we can inspire each other, at home and in our travels, with love, friendship, and appreciation in our hearts for the many creative ways in which Humanity can live.

Acknowledgements

I first wish to acknowledge certain people who have been supportive and influential to me over the years, as they relate to this work:

My late twin brother, artist Vance A. Larson: For the entirety of our lives we worked together, usually from a great distance, with the vision to publish his art and my writings. One of his earliest paintings, which gives the reader a sense of the great beauty and vision of his work, is shown in the book's Conclusion.

I am also indebted to my late father, John Bertrand Larson; my late mother, Shirley Glynn Lockwood Larson; and my late ex-husband, Major General Fred E. Haynes, USMC. I was incredibly fortunate to have these three ethical and brilliant people in my life as mentors.

I am also grateful to my late older brother, Mark John Larson, who was severely brain damaged from his baby vaccines. Looking back at our lives, it was Mark's injury that set me on the path of always questioning the status quo and seeking alternatives.

I also wish to acknowledge some gifted artists and Illume colleagues who have been especially supportive of my work: Walter Gurbo, the late Betty Ann Fraley, the late Alberta Hutchinson, the late Jane Evelynne Higgins and her husband Timothy Main, and Marjory Harris, all of whom contributed to the book's beautiful art. I also thank Jerry Rudnitsky and Ginnah Howard for their supportive assistance, Kip Ayers for his empowering cover, and Cristian Radu for his beautiful book design.

I also wish to thank several other friends for their assistance: Entrepreneurs and authors Dean Roberts, Swami Tirtha, and Subhamoy Das; antique motor vehicle restorer Jon Crim, who gave me helpful information about vintage vehicles; and writer Jeff Davidson, who, back in the 1980s, introduced me to the Fritz *Technologies for Creating* course, which taught extraordinarily helpful techniques for manifesting one's vision.

Throughout the writing of *Creative Provinces* I was, in particular, influenced in my direction by the works of countless creative and performing visionaries. And every day I meet people who show me visions of the many possibilities of how we can live. This has led me to deeply understand and appreciate that *we are all artists*—from the builder to the dressmaker, from the homemaker to the chef, from the farmer to the gardener, from the singer to the designer, from the helper to the planner—working together to create our magnificent world.

Thank you to everyone.

About the Author

Valerie Haynes, pictured in front of Vance A. Larson's painting, *The Lifestar* (Photo by Walter Gurbo)

Valerie Ann Larson Haynes studied political science at the University of Connecticut and began her career as an officer in the U.S. Marine Corps, then as a professional staff member of the U. S. House of Representatives Armed Services Committee. She later became an independent writer, editor, and publisher in the arts and sciences. She is the author of *Doctor Goldbunny—A Modern Fable* (Illume 2011), and *New Colors—Poetic Creations and Paintings of Valerie Haynes and Vance A. Larson* (Illume 2025), and is the founding editor of the cooperative publishing group, Illume Writers & Artists.

    Having a lifelong interest in organizing people to manifest their visions, Valerie has been active in numerous groups to help people publish, perform, and display their works.

www.ingramcontent.com/pod-product-compliance
Lightning Source LLC
Chambersburg PA
CBHW060946050426
42337CB00052B/1601